JANET PYWELL

# The Influencers

*A Ronda George Thriller – Book 2*

*'Whether one believes in a religion or not, and whether one believes*
*in rebirth or not, there isn't anyone who doesn't appreciate kindness and compassion.'*
*Dalai Lama*

# Foreword

**The Influencers**
*Book 2*

A Ronda George Thriller
Talented kickboxer and *Masterchef* turns detective.

*After a shattering discovery – will Ronda survive?*

Charismatic TV personality Daniel Clarkson employs Ronda George to cater at an exclusive function in his well-known Kent country pub.

She's shocked to find her ex, James Frampton, who stole her savings, is launching a new cryptocurrency.

With the help of eight wealthy, social influencers it will take the Internet by storm.

But Ronda discovers that the business deal is a scam. James and his business partners will stop at nothing to launch the venture - even if it means silencing her forever.

Ronda's intuition and instincts kick in and she calls on her army and martial arts skills in order to survive and get back what's rightfully hers.

The *Influencers* is the second book in the Ronda George series of thrillers which can be read and enjoyed in any order, although it's exciting to watch Ronda's personal development with each book in the series and it's preferable to read them in sequence.

For fans of female sleuths and aficionados of Lucy Foley, Catherine Cooper, Allie Reynolds, Shari Lapena, Riley Sager and Lisa Jewell. You will be instantly hooked.

# 1

# Chapter 1

*'One must pass through the network of influence. One is obligated to be influenced, and one accepts this influence very naturally. From the start, one doesn't realize this. The first thing to know: one doesn't realize one is influenced. One thinks he is already liberated, and one is far from it!'*
**Marcel Duchamp**

The autumn downpour takes me by surprise, and heavy rain is trickling down my neck. I'm juggling the front door key, balancing my shopping, including tonight's dinner of lamb kebabs, and Molly's lead, when my mobile rings. I push open the door, and Molly tugs herself free. She's excited to be home, knocks against my leg and I lose my balance and my grip. My shopping drops on the floor. The fresh brown eggs smash on the concrete step.

'Hello?'

'Ronda George?' The stranger's voice is formal and shows signs of an expensive education.

'Yes.'

'Daniel Clarkson, we haven't met. I'm—'

I know precisely who Daniel Clarkson is. He's one of the most well-known celebrities you could imagine, a face for TV: chiselled jaw, sculpted cheekbones and, even dimples. He's the nation's favourite host. He's successfully narrated a series of documentary TV programmes from rail travel across the globe to unusual gardens in Bolivia.

'I hope you don't mind me calling you, but the thing is, I own a pub in the heart of the Kent countryside ...' I hear the proud smile in his voice.

His pub, The Cockerel and the Guinea Pig is legendary. It's booked up months in advance, and it's almost impossible to get a table reservation. Tina and I have tried on many occasions since it opened three years ago, and in the end we gave up. It's often in the *Hello!* magazine with celebrity couples posing outside with their fast, flashy cars.

I'm speechless.

Daniel Clarkson is calling me.

'The thing is,' he continues in his melodic TV voice, 'my regular chef is ill, and I have a crucially important function to cater for, and I was wondering if you'd be free.'

I glance at the mess oozing out of the paper bag—the sticky eggs leaking over the doorstep. Molly stands looking hopefully at the lamb, so I nudge her away with my knee and pick it up.

I glance back into the quiet London street. It's a haven of peace in the busy metropolis, and I'm wondering if I'm on some reality show. A celebrity set-up where a reporter suddenly appears laughing saying, '*we fooled you*', and you feel an absolute idiot while trying to smile for the cameras.

'Ronda? Are you there?'

'Yes, I am. Sorry.'

'I did see you on *Masterchef.* How many years ago was that?'

'Almost three.'

'My goodness, was it really?'

I close my eyes and rub my temple as flashing images of my life fill my head: the fame, the recognition, the media attention, the fun and laughter. Then the best part – the hard work – the challenge and the success when I was recognised for my skill and artistry in the kitchen. I was happy then, but that was before James and his betrayal—

'Have I caught you at a bad time, Ronda?'

Inside, waiting at the end of the hallway, Molly is now in her downward dog pose, tail wagging, waiting for her breakfast. She barks. It's a small yap to remind me she's had a long walk and she's hungry.

'No, it's fine.'

He hesitates, and then he gives a small embarrassed laugh.

'Um, well. Perhaps it's not something you'd like to do then?'

I'd be crazy to turn him down. It's the chance of a lifetime, to work with one of the most well-known, and revered masters of television. It's also the opportunity of a lifetime to resurrect my flailing career. Apart from catering for a wealthy German businessman a few months ago in Scotland, I can't seem to get my business kick-started again – or my confidence. This is what I need.

'I'm sorry I bothered you, Ronda. It's just that—'

'Sorry, no, no. Daniel, I'd love to. It would be a pleasure.'

Did I really call him Daniel with such familiarity?

'Great, that's fantastic.' He sounds genuinely pleased.

'Yes, I'm sorry. I know I should sound far more enthusiastic, less star-struck,' I admit with a smile that I wish he could see, and I'm rewarded with his throaty laugh. I warm to the theme and add, 'It's very kind of you to think of me. Let me check my calendar.'

I slam the front door with my foot, leaving the mess of the uncooked scrambled eggs on the step and I lean with my back against the front door. It's beginning to dawn on me, I'm speaking to Daniel Clarkson, and he wants me to cook in his famous pub.

'When is it for?' I ask.

'Well, unfortunately, it *is* short notice. It's for this Wednesday.'

I push past Molly who can't believe I'm doing something more important than feeding her. She jumps up and puts her muddy paws on my jacket. I push her off, throw the lamb on the kitchen counter and reach for my diary. I check the date knowing my diary is empty.

'The first Wednesday in November?' I ask.

'Yes.'

'Um, I think I could juggle that around ....' I pretend. 'That would be fine, Daniel. I'll pop it in my diary.'

He breathes a solemn and dramatic sigh.

'Thank goodness for that,' he gushes. 'I thought you were going to turn me down, Ronda. You certainly know how to keep a man on his toes.'

I hear the smile in his voice, and I realise it's what makes him successful. It's what they call *charisma*, and it's what I'm lacking. After ten years in the British Army, I haven't developed these skills. Fortunately, in the kitchen, I can be monosyllabic and grumpy if I want to be, so long as I work in a team. I can lose myself in my profession as a chef. How I won *Masterchef*, or why I was so popular still remains a mystery to me.

'It's all pretty straightforward,' he explains. 'The guests are arriving at midday. They'll have coffee or aperitifs and then lunch at one-thirty.'

'That's fine.' I make a note in my diary.

'Erm, they're an international crowd. There are a few people you may recognise, you know, a few celebrities, a politician and even a prince but I'm sure you will be discreet.'

'Of course.'

I don't add that fame or the celebrity lifestyle doesn't interest me and that I'm more into good manners and kindness.

'The thing is, Ronda, no one must know about this meeting, this gathering. You will have to sign a waiver, a declaration, not to speak about it. It's standard practice in this situation. These people don't want to have their lives splashed all over the press.'

*Unless it suits them and you want the* Hello! *magazine all over your pub*, I want to add, but I say aloud, 'That's fine.'

'I guess you've signed something before when you've cooked for royalty?'

'Yes, something similar,' I reply.

That's why he wants me. He's heard that I've cooked for Charles and Camilla on several occasions. It's something I never speak about, but the word does get out, and I'm not complaining. After winning *Masterchef*, I'd been very successful; jetting all over the world to cook for private functions in exotic locations, for pop stars, billionaires, philanthropists, business people and even royalty. It had been thrilling, exciting and fun; however, that was over a year ago – before I lost everything – before James took everything, including my confidence.

'Good. Good. I'm delighted, Ronda. Well, I won't take up any more of your time. I'm sure you're a very busy woman. I'll send you an email confirming it all, your remuneration and, of course, the non-disclosure agreement.'

'Perfect.'

'If you have any questions just email me.'

'What about the menu?'

'It will be straightforward, very low key.'

'How many guests?'

'Eight.'

I stare at Molly, who sits watching me patiently. She's giving me her Paddington hard stare, to get me off the phone quickly.

'Eight?' I scribble down the number in my empty diary. I know that afterwards, in my excitement, I won't remember a word of what Daniel's said and I suddenly can't wait to tell Tina.

He continues, 'I'll send you the menu suggestions. I'll purchase everything fresh the day before, and I'll send you a list. If you come down early on Wednesday morning and there's anything else you need, I can always get someone to pop out and get it for you. Does that sound, alright?'

'You don't want me to suggest a menu?'

'No, not at all. The host is quite particular. I'll email you now with the details, and I'll see you on Wednesday. I'll send you directions to my place. It should only take an hour from your home.'

'You know where I live?' He doesn't answer so I say, 'Can I ask how you got my phone number and who recommended me?'

He pauses before answering.

'A very good friend, someone who thinks very highly of you.'

Tina, my best friend, is an international criminal lawyer but she would have warned me. She'd have given me the heads up that Daniel was going to phone me, besides, she's probably never even met Daniel Clarkson. So, who else could it be? I wonder if it's any of my old army companions, but I doubt it would be anyone who wouldn't forewarn me.

Molly sits at my feet, looking hopeful.

'Thinks highly of me,' I reply automatically.

'Yes, James Frampton recommended you,' Daniel says softly in my ear.

'James?' I whisper.

'Yes, he speaks very highly of you. He said that you were the one.'

My knees give way, and I slump onto the kitchen chair. My mouth is dry, and my hands are shaking. My stomach turns and lifts as if I'm on a rollercoaster and I think I may be sick.

Molly regards me warily, pads closer and then places her head on my knee, as if she's aware of my sudden distress.

'James?' I mumble.

'He'll be thrilled to know you've agreed.'

James. I feel my anger igniting. My shock has turned to fire and outrage. How dare James speak about me? I never want to see or hear from him again. I don't want anything to do with him, but I *do* want my money back. My money that he stole from me last February – almost nine months ago.

'But, he won't be as delighted as me,' Daniel purrs. 'I'm looking forward to it already.'

How has my ex managed to get me hooked up to cater for a group of celebrities?

Does James know Daniel? When did he even meet him?

'See you on Wednesday,' Daniel croons. 'And, Ronda?' He pauses.

'Yes.'

'I'm really looking forward to meeting you. I've heard so

much about you.'

He hangs up, and I realise it's too late to change my mind.

Why has James, a man I dated for two years, who stole my money and left me standing like an idiot at the registry office on my wedding day, recommended me for this job when he hasn't even answered my phone calls?

* * *

Tina sits opposite me at my small kitchen table, drinking wine. It's a dark and dismal afternoon, but there's something magical and melancholy in the air, so I haven't closed the plantation shutters. The window overlooks the patio at the back of my basement flat and although it's early November the mushroom-shaped garden lights shine in wistfulness as though they're small homes for garden gnomes.

Inside my two-bedroomed flat, it's cosy and warm. Molly sits dozing on her bed in the corner by the oven. She's given up watching us and hoping for the crumbs from our table, and now her head rests on her paws, and she's snoring gently.

Tina reaches for the Rioja bottle and tops up our glasses.

'That was delicious, Ronda. You certainly haven't lost your touch.'

'It's only a Sunday supper,' I reply.

She smiles. 'You're so modest. I couldn't cook lamb like that with that gorgeous crusted coat, and those rosemary and garlic potatoes were delicious...'

'And I couldn't be a criminal lawyer.'

'Horses for courses,' she adds flippantly, dismissing her essential job at one of the most prestigious law firms in the country.

8

I put our empty plates on the kitchen counter, sit at the table and pull my wine glass closer, holding it in both hands as if it will warm me.

Tina wraps her blonde hair behind her ears, revealing her heart-shaped face, and places a slim hand under her dimpled chin.

'So, let's cut to the chase, Ronda. You've told me about Daniel and James recommending you for the job on Wednesday but you've been avoiding the issue of last summer. You haven't told me properly why you turned down working with Inspector Joachin.'

I frown, thinking about my experience last August in Scotland.

'That was ages ago.'

'I know. You told me all about the weekend and the handsome Hugo and everything that happened, but then you said you'd decided not to work with them, why?'

I stare at Tina, remembering how I'd travelled to Aberdeen to cater for a fiftieth birthday weekend celebration. It hadn't turned out at all as I expected, I'd agreed to be the eyes and ears for an inspector from Europol, and I'd never expected it would involve a stolen and valuable blue diamond ring and an unsolved murder from five years ago.

It had ended with me travelling back on the train to London with Hugo. He'd been the sommelier for the weekend as well as an undercover policeman. And, under his disguise, he'd kissed me. The trouble was, I thought he'd meant it, and it had been confusing. Afterwards, when I realised he'd kissed me in the line of duty, I'd been furious with him and myself. I had refused to speak to him. I'd also been so exhausted after all the excitement of the weekend that I'd fallen asleep for most of the train journey back to London. He'd woken me halfway with a tepid cup of coffee from the buffet car, and a chocolate bar and I'd eaten it sulkily, hardly speaking. He'd tried to talk, but I needed space. I had to get my head around everything that had happened. All I could think of right now was James and how he had betrayed me. I was determined I wasn't falling for that all over again.

'Well?' Tina prompts.

'I didn't want to become an undercover informer – or helper, as he called it.'

Tina smiles. It's a smile I know well. It's one that says, '*there's more to it than you're telling me, but I'll be patient.*'

She sits waiting, watching me and expecting more of a response, and I imagine this is how she is with her clients.

I continue, 'It's not what I do, Tina. You might have an urgent passion for saving the world, or for putting criminals behind bars or whatever it is, but I don't. Not after ten years in the army. I just want to cook. I want to stay away from people and make tasty, delicious and original dishes. I want to use my creativity. Nothing more and nothing less. I don't want to spy on people.' I wave my wineglass with emphasis.

'It's not spying,' she argues.

'Being someone's eyes and ears *is* spying. And, besides, if I have to be with awful people like that family in Scotland again, then I'm definitely not interested. Besides, I wasn't even good at it.'

Tina grins. 'You found a rare and valuable diamond and solved a murder. I'd call that pretty good.'

'It was a fluke. And, besides, I didn't do it single-handedly.'

'Oh, that's true, who was the French policeman you liked?'

'Hugo? I didn't like him.'

Tina throws her head back and laughs. 'That's what you say.'

'I'm off men. I told you. I'm not interested, not after what James did to me.'

'Didn't you go and see James's mother?'

'Yes, I plucked up the courage a few weeks ago, and I told her very gently that her son owed me money. I told her that he took all my savings and that I was bankrupt.'

'What did she say?'

I reach across to hold Tina's hand, and I stare into her eyes. 'She leaned over the table. She took my hand, like this, and looked me in the eyes and said, *'Oh, James wouldn't do that. He wouldn't hurt you. He wouldn't do it deliberately. He's not like that'*.'

I place Tina's hand back on the table and continue, 'I wanted to scream at her and tell her that he's a liar and a cheat, and a ...,' I pause, fumbling for the right words, but I shake my head in frustration. 'But I didn't say anything, Tina. I just left. She had no intention of speaking to him. She didn't believe me. She wouldn't hear a word said against her son. So she was never going to help me get my money back.'

'Well, maybe the fact that he's recommended you for this job on Wednesday is a step in the right direction. Maybe he's trying to help you. Have you called him?'

'I tried a few times, but it still clicks to voicemail.'

'Did you leave a message?'

'Yes, and it wasn't polite.'

'Do you think James will be there on Wednesday?'

'No way. He wouldn't be hobnobbing with royalty or politicians. He doesn't mix in those types of social circles. The last time I saw him, he was knocking on doors like a two-bit salesman with some software he was trying to sell that he'd stolen from someone else. You know what he's like. He's a conman.'

'Good. Well, at least you'll be able to relax and have fun. And, you never know, Daniel is a real charmer. He's good-looking too.'

'Besides, James is probably wrapped around some tart in the Caribbean – a woman he's conned into lending him money and—'

'Lending?' Tina snorts.

'Well, exactly, I mean stolen. I haven't given up. I'll get my money somehow.'

'Maybe you can get some more information out of Daniel on Wednesday?'

'That's what I was thinking. I'll try, but James has been as elusive as the Scarlet Pimpernel. I'll probably never see him again. If Daniel can give me a different phone number for him, then I might stand a chance of finding him at last.'

'What will you do, hound him?'

'I want my money, Tina. It was bad enough that he stole my dreams, my hope, my love and well, just about everything, but it's my money that I want back now. I'll do what it takes.' I drain my wineglass. 'Come on, let's take Molly out and get some fresh air or I'll drink too much and start moaning about James again. You can tell me all about Graham. When is he moving in?'

Tina stands up, straightens her skirt and reaches for her jacket. 'It's early days yet.'

'Yeah, yeah, you've had your eye on him for two years.'

'We're colleagues.'

'And you're both single.'

'I'm not rushing things.'

12

'Have you cooked for him yet?'

'Goodness, no. He'd never want to see me again.' Tina laughs. 'So, tell me, what's on the menu on Wednesday?'

I shake my head dismissively, and it makes her laugh.

'What?' she asks.

'Prawn cocktail, steak and chips, or chicken in tamarind sauce.'

'What's wrong with that?'

'Well, it's not the most adventurous meal. It's out of the eighties. I hope Daniel's not stringing me along, but he has sent me a disclaimer to sign, and it all seems above board. He also told me they are very well-known people and there's a prince, and—'

'And, you think this isn't the finest fare for royalty?'

'I'm thinking, if this is a wind-up and someone is wasting my time, they could end up dead.'

Tina laughs and claps her hands. It's probably not the best reaction for a criminal lawyer, but then she says, 'How lovely. The perfect murder. Chop chop, pop him in a stewing pot...'

I pick up a knife, and I re-enact Alfred Hitchcock's famous movie scene in *Psycho*, the stabbing in the shower, and I cry, '*Eek, eek, eek.*'

Molly stretches and yawns.

# 2

# Chapter 2

*'If you want to influence people, you want them to accept your suggestions, you don't say, 'You don't know how to use the English language,' or 'How could you make that argument?' It will be welcomed much more if you have a gentle touch than if you are aggressive.'*
**Ruth Bader Ginsburg**

The drive to Daniel's pub in the Kent countryside is under an hour in my new red, convertible. It's a Fiat 500 that I call Peanut. It's nothing flashy, but I love it. It's easy to park in London, and it's fun to put down the roof in the summer. It's also affordable.

Last August, after the job in Aberdeen, I was also given a substantial and welcome bonus from Inspector Joachin. He said the original owner, of the blue diamond ring, a sultan, was grateful for my help and he wanted to reward me for my efforts. Fortunately, this was a timely act. Since then, my bank balance has improved, and so has my confidence. However, I knew it would take a while for my career to resurrect itself and, as I drive, I imagine the possibilities of expanding my catering business once again.

Who are the eight celebrities?

Buying a second-hand car seemed like a good idea in the summer with the roof down and Molly panting happily beside me, but now it's windy on the motorway. The rain has stopped, and the car's buffeted against the wind. Once I turn off the main road, into a pretty, meandering country road, I'm in the undulating Kent countryside – known as the Garden of England. The ripeness of the summer has turned the fields to deep shades and colourful autumnal hues of brown, orange and amber. Leaves have been ripped from the trees that now bend as their branches bow across the road, waving like the Queen. I respond with a cheeky wave wondering if I'm going a little crazy. But even if I am, I feel myself relaxing, and I'm excited about cooking again for important guests and the possibilities that may arise in the future.

I'm tempted to call Tina, who is working from home today and looking after Molly. She said she was happy to walk her to the park mid-morning and I know Molly will be sleeping after our early run.

I brake hard. Check my rear-view mirror and reverse. I almost missed the turning. The lane narrows and the fields surrounding me are filled with hop frames and apple trees, reminding me that this is real ale and cider country.

Then I catch sight of The Cockerel and the Guinea Pig sign, swinging in the breeze. The pub is set back from the road, and it's everything an English pub should be; thatched roof, leaded-light windows and, even at this time of year, there are well-tended window boxes full of red geraniums. Although it's early morning, a waft of smoke is already rising from the chimney.

To the left and right, the grounds are stunning. Lawns and gardens are meticulous; pretty wooden tables, barrels filled with greenery and autumn colours – it's tasteful, decorative and welcoming.

It also looks expensive.

I turn the car onto the gravel drive and follow it around to the back of the building, as per my instructions on Daniel's email, although it's natural for me to look for the kitchen door, the tradesman's entrance. I park beside an imposing black Porsche Cayenne, and I'm pretty sure Peanut would fit into its boot. I haven't even turned off the engine when a man comes striding out of the back door, smiling and waving. To my delight, Daniel Clarkson looks much more handsome in real life than on television.

* * *

'Ronda, welcome. It's delightful to meet you at long last.'

I climb out of the car, and I'm about to hold out my hand when he moves effortlessly and, taking me by the shoulders, kisses me on both cheeks. He stands back to appraise me, and I'm pleased I've taken the time this morning to add makeup and lipstick to my weary face.

He smiles. 'It's an early start, I know. Thank you, Ronda. I'm pleased you're here. Come in, come in.'

Although I'm only here for the day, I pull out my weekend bag with my change of clothes and kitchen knives from the passenger seat.

'Let me take that.' He ushers me in by the elbow, carrying my bag, smiling happily, asking me about my journey from London and if I know Kent.

'I was thinking of opening a restaurant on the coast, in Whitstable.'

'Ah, lovely choice. Fresh oysters.'

I smile. I don't tell him that was before James ran off with my savings. I'd been planning to open a small restaurant in the seaside town and fulfil a dream.

He waves his arm grandly around the kitchen.

'This is it.' He places my bag on the floor. 'Make yourself at home.'

'It's beautiful,' I say, and while Daniel points out the obvious – fridge, hot plates, grill, pots and pans – I'm distracted by his energy and appearance.

He's undoubtedly attractive, maybe ten years older than me, in his early forties with greying hair that in a few years will be called salt and pepper. He's assertive, strong without looking too muscular, and his dark eyes are probing, not intense. He wears a casual and expensive navy suit, crisp white shirt and red tie. He looks like a successful, prosperous and confident businessman but he has the charm of a TV celebrity; naturally talkative, interested without being personal, curious without being interrogative.

We chat easily and I take everything in. Daniel is an excellent host. After a look around the kitchen, he prepares coffee and we leave it to percolate while he takes me through to the bar area. It's quaint, characteristically beautiful and old-fashioned. There's a long bar with crystal glasses overhead and pristine bottles on the shelves behind, shining, welcoming and inviting.

It's a typical English country pub that you would dream about on an autumn day, such as this. It's rustic yet comfortable, polished yet natural and although the furniture is dark wood, it's not claustrophobic. Warm lamps, cosy seating and comfortable chairs make it seem deceptively spacious. There are several smaller, cosy, private nooks for romantic meals, and colourful lights and used wine bottles with burnt candle wax. The log fire sizzling in the grate, spitting and cracking, makes me feel as though I want to curl up and lie on a sofa with a good book for the day instead of working in the kitchen.

Daniel walks me to the end of the bar and guides me down a corridor, passing the toilets, to the back of the pub. He stands aside to allow me to enter first through the double doors. It's a discreet room, hidden, but when he opens the doors, I'm speechless. It breathtaking. This room is decorated in warm colours: gold, red and amber. Damask curtains hang heavily at the long glass doors, which I guess in summer would open onto a private outside dining area where there's a patio, a stone wall and a barbecue.

Today, there is a log fire prepared in the grate but not yet lit. An assortment of harvested fruits and vegetables is on display in an old cart in the corner and in the opposite corner is a small but well-stocked bar with three special temperature fridges. At a glance, I'd say they house rare and expensive wines. In the centre of the room, a large round table that could easily seat twelve people is laid for eight places. Cutlery, alongside the appropriate wine glass or goblet for each of the three courses, is polished and ready and in the centre of the table is a discreet autumn decoration; a wooden log with beautiful fresh sunflowers.

The furniture is a mixture of old and new, worn and comfortable, inviting and also very expensive. High beams and long windows allow in light and give the room a feeling of space.

'Well?' he asks.

I blink.

'Sorry, I was taking it all in. It's absolutely beautiful.'

'Thank you. I'm very proud of it.'

'Is this part of the pub a barn conversion?'

He nods. 'It was a marathon project. When I bought it six years ago, it was a rundown old pub with rotting wood and a cellar that flooded every winter. It took over a year to sort it all, but we got there in the end.'

'We?'

'My wife Jenny and I.'

'Ah.'

I hadn't known about her. She is never mentioned on television.

'We're divorced now,' he adds.

'I'm sorry.'

He smiles and shakes his head. 'These things happen. Come and see this.'

I follow him across the room, past the cart with harvested vegetables, to a door which he opens like a magician about to reveal his final trick.

'This is a short cut to the kitchen. You can cut across this hallway, and we're back in the kitchen.'

'Wow, that's great.'

'It's good for the staff and for serving food. You don't have to pass through the bar each time.'

'Where does that passageway lead to?' I nod to an outside door.

'Well, that way—' he nods to the left '—leads to the bar but this door is a private entrance for our special guests. Not all of them want to walk through the bar and the restaurant. They don't want to be seen by the regulars so they can come in and out at the back of the pub. Come and see. They park around here.'

I follow him to the porch and realise my car is parked further to the left, nearer the kitchen door. Had I continued driving around the building to the back, I would have come to this entrance.

We stand on the step, and there's a magnificent view across the open fields, and I take a while to absorb the natural beauty of the setting.

He waves in the opposite direction, toward the road at the front of the pub.

'Our regular customers park at the front. This is used for our special guests as you will see later. '

'That's an incredible view.'

He turns to look over his shoulder as if he's forgotten what it looks like. 'I have an arrangement with the local farmer that the choppers can land there, as long as I let him know in advance, and he can move the sheep. As I said, it's for the guests who don't want to come by road.'

I nod as if I mix with them all the time.

'Now, you'd probably love a coffee, wouldn't you, Ronda?'

I smile. I like Daniel. I appreciate his manners, his attentiveness and his kindness. And, I'm suddenly quite comfortable knowing I don't have to stretch myself today. It's not my menu. All I have to do is to make it look and taste delicious. It's not a problematic menu. Today will be a doddle and, looking at Daniel's warm smile, great fun.

Daniel's hand rests briefly on my waist as he guides me through the short cut, back into the kitchen. I'm not offended by his closeness. He feels warm, safe and secure, and I'm suddenly excited to be here.

* * *

It's nine o'clock, and we're on our second cup of coffee, still sitting at a small round table in the corner of the kitchen.

'I have a proper office upstairs,' Daniel explains. 'But it's sometimes easier to sit and chat here, or in the pub of course.'

'Do you live here?'

He looks surprised. 'No, no, there is a one-bedroom flat upstairs, but it's quite small. Sometimes Ronald, my regular chef, stays there but now he's put his back out and he's at home with his family in Broadstairs.'

We have the menu spread before us, and occasionally Daniel gets up and shows me the produce he bought from the local market this morning.

'Freshly picked.' He holds out a tray of mushrooms. 'The woods are full of them. And, apples, you couldn't have a dessert without apples – not around here – it would be sacrilege.' He grins. 'And, I believe no one makes a traditional apple pie like you.'

I smile. It was one of my signature dishes on *Masterchef*, and since then it has been one of my most popular desserts, especially with my home-made vanilla ice cream or my infamous home-made Baileys.

We spend a few minutes talking about the show, television, fame and careers, and I realise that for all Daniel's money and success, he's very like me. He appreciates the notoriety but admits it can be short-lived.

'You'll only be on TV for as long as the public wants you. Have you ever thought of making a TV programme?'

I smile. 'There was talk of it but, to be honest, it's not me. I enjoy the flexibility of travelling around and taking my recipes and skills with me.'

He stares at me.

'Ronda, I'm not hitting on you, but you have the most amazing and unusual green eyes.'

'Thank you.' I turn away.

'You've probably been told that lots of times?'

'I was often told I was like my mother.'

'She must be an attractive woman.'

'Yes, but she passed away seventeen years ago.' I pick up the coffee pot sitting between us on the table, not because I want more coffee but to distract me from his scrutiny.

'The thing is,' he says, leaning across the table, closer to me, 'It's not how much you earn or how famous you are, Ronda. It's about keeping your feet firmly planted on the ground, isn't it?'

I nod. I'm now holding my china coffee mug in both hands and I regard him over the rim.

He continues, 'I know footballers, actors, singers, you name it, they've all flocked here over the past few years. They all want to be seen but so few of them are gracious. They forget where they've come from and they forget what it's like to be normal. They've got used to being treated like stars. They don't do their own washing. They don't lift a vacuum and they certainly don't dust.' He waves his arms dramatically and it makes me laugh. 'They're used to the best things in life; the fastest car, the biggest hotel room, the most glamorous partner – nothing is ever enough.'

I smile thinking of his Porsche Cayenne parked outside and the amount he must have spent to renovate this pub.

I glance at my watch.

'Sorry, am I holding you back? It's so good to chat with you,

Ronda.'

'I'd like to make a start if that's okay?'

'Yes of course.'

I stand up, and he stands up too. He's slightly taller than me. His lips are full, and his aftershave is expensively sophisticated. I'm trying to identify the expensive spicy aroma when he says, 'I know you're a stickler for time management, is that from your army training days?'

I must look surprised because he bursts out laughing.

'I haven't offended you, have I?'

'Not at all,' I reply.

Ten years in the army is hard to forget. It instilled in me basic training including survival, how to use a rifle, field craft skills and first aid which has come in handy in the kitchen for wounds like burns and cuts. It's also been excellent training for the five basic but necessary skills that make a good chef: the ability to work in a team, multitasking, attention to detail, the ability to handle criticism and even creativity. For me, imagination is the soul for creating new ideas and taking risks – trying something new. It inspires food tastes and presentation. It's quite simply, my passion.

I move away, not wanting to engage in a conversation about my past but he moves with me to the kitchen counter.

'You served abroad?'

'Yes.'

'In the Army Catering Corps?'

'Yes.'

'In combat zones?'

'Sometimes.' I reach for my bag and pull out my special leather roll of Japanese knives, trying to block out the memories.

'Are these your knives?'

'Of course.'

'Good. Good. Well ...'

'I'll get started then.'

I want him to go away and leave me alone, but he stands resolutely in the same spot looking at me as if he wants to unfold the complicated layers of thoughts in my head.

'Well,' he says again. 'You'll have some help arriving shortly. Billy is our sous-chef, and Daisy is our apprentice in the kitchen, but she can also help us wait on the tables today.'

'Us?' I glance at him, intrigued that he'd get his hands dirty and collect dishes.

He grins apologetically and explains, 'You see, Steph and Jess are my normal waiting staff, but this is a very private function, so I've cut back on them. It's just the essential people here today.'

'What about the main restaurant? How many covers are you expecting?'

Daniel looks blank. 'Sorry, Ronda. I should have explained. I've closed the pub today. There is no one else, only our eight guests.'

'Oh, right. That makes it easier.' I grin to cover my stupidity. I had assumed it would be a regular kitchen all day and I'm suddenly flustered. With the rate Daniel is paying me to prepare just one meal for eight people, I would have cooked all week for a full pub.

'You'll probably recognise some of the guests from television or the news. That's why I asked you to sign the non-disclosure agreement. No one must know about this meeting today, Ronda. I can't stress enough just how secret this is.'

'That's no problem.' I reach for my bag. 'I'll just pop to the bathroom and change into my whites then I can get started.'

He steps aside, and that's when the back door opens, and a flurry of cold air spins into the room like a chilly whirlwind. I turn around expecting Billy or Daisy, but it's not them at all. His dark hair has grown a little longer, his chestnut eyes are still mesmerising, and he's as handsome as I remember him from last August when we stepped off the train together in London from Aberdeen.

'Hello.' Hugo grins from the doorway 'What a great place for an English pub. This is lovely, Daniel.'

'Ah, come in, come in, Hugo. Good to see you.'

Daniel moves quickly to usher Hugo inside and shake his hand. 'This is Ronda, our culinary chef for today. Ronda, this is Hugo – our sommelier.'

Hugo grins. 'Hello, Ronda.'

'Have you met before?' Daniel asks.

Before I can speak Hugo replies with his mouth turned down in denial.

'No, never, but it's lovely to meet you.' Hugo reaches for my hand and he shakes it firmly before adding, 'I've heard so much about you, Ronda. I'm a big fan of *Masterchef*.'

# 3

# Chapter 3

*'Man's nature is not essentially evil. Brute nature has been known to yield to the influence of love. You must never despair of human nature.'*
**Mahatma Gandhi**

I'm standing in the ladies' toilet. It's tucked away at the back of the bar. Aside from the three cubicles, the dressing room has three mirrors and dressing tables with freshly picked orange gerbera and white Asiatic lilies. The room is carpeted in rich burgundy. It's luxurious and comfortable. It's also probably half the size of my entire London flat.

I pull on my checked trousers, fasten them at the waist and check my appearance in the full-length mirror. I sigh, puffing out my cheeks and pouting. Hugo's presence has put a different slant on the day. My earlier enthusiasm and excitement has evaporated, and now I feel alert and strangely tense.

What is Hugo doing here?

I pull on a clean white tunic over my navy vest. My heart is racing, and my fingers feel too big to secure the front buttons.

I curse and eventually fasten the top button, but my hands are shaking.

How could he do this to me?

I rummage in my bag and find my trademark bandana. Today I've chosen a green, gold, yellow and orange one. I wrap it around my head, leaving my spiky hair poking out at the top.

Is Hugo here on business as a sommelier, or is he here with Inspector Joachin?

I pout my lips in the mirror, add bright purple lipstick, then I stand back and take a look at myself.

'You'll do, Ronda George.'

I pull my mobile from my pocket and stand by the sash window, overlooking the courtyard at the side of the pub. Parked beside my Fiat 500 and the Porsche Cayenne is a dark blue Audi. I tap my fingernail on the window and wait, listening to the ring tone and when it's answered,

'Tina?' I whisper.

'Ronda? Hi, are you alright?' she replies quickly.

'Yes.' I turn my back on the door and rest my head on the pane of glass. 'Hugo is here.'

'Hugo? The sommelier?'

'Yes.'

'Why?'

'I don't know. He's pretending we haven't met.'

She pauses before replying, 'Then you must do the same.'

'I have.'

Tina sighs heavily. 'So, what's it all about?'

'I have no idea.'

'You'll have to be careful.'

'I will.

'Who are the guests?'

'Daniel hasn't said.'

'Have you asked?'

'No.'

'Goodness, Ronda. I have no idea why Inspector Joachin would want you on his team; you don't find anything out. That's the first thing I'd want to know.'

'I'm here to cook,' I hiss. 'I'm not Miss bloody Marple.'

Tina stifles a laugh. 'I have to go. I'm in a meeting.'

'And you're talking to me?'

'Yeah, you're on loudspeaker!'

I giggle despite myself. I know she's joking and it breaks the tension across my neck and shoulders.

'Just make sure you don't poison anyone, Ronda,' Tina adds, 'Maybe you meeting up with Hugo is fate. Maybe you're destined to be together, forever,' she croons.

I groan dramatically with displeasure. 'That doesn't even dignify an answer.'

'Call me when you're home and if it's not too late, I'll pop round. And, be careful, Ronda.'

'I will. I promise.' I end the call and drop the phone into my tunic pocket.

'Hi.'

Startled I jump. I turn around, and there's a curly mop of hair and a mischievous face peering from behind the open bathroom door.

'Sorry, did I frighten you? You must be Ronda.' She smiles.

'Yes.'

'I'm Daisy, the apprentice. You're going to be showing me everything today.'

'Great.' I wonder how long she's been there for and if she listened to my entire conversation.

\* \* \*

Daisy waits for me. She insists I look amazing, and she loves my colourful bandana and did I make it myself, and she wasn't eavesdropping, and she didn't hear my phone conversation. She saw the final of *Masterchef* on TV and she wanted me to win. It was just the best thing that she ever saw and it changed her life. She can't wait to cook with me.

'Would it be okay to take a selfie with you?'

We're still in the bathroom, so I nod.

She stands beside me, lengthens her arm and points the camera at us both.

'I can't believe I'm cooking with you today, Ronda. Troy, my little brother, usually does the washing up but Billy and I are doing everything today.'

'How old is Troy?'

'He's nineteen. I'm twenty-one.'

'Daniel only wants Billy and me; even the waiting staff aren't here.'

'Come on, let's go,' I say, opening the bathroom door, eager to escape her persistent questions.

'Aren't you excited?' she asks.

'No.'

As we enter the kitchen, Daniel and Hugo look up. They're standing at the corner table looking at the paperwork on the table.

'I thought we'd frightened you off,' Daniel says pleasantly. 'So I asked Daisy to check on you. I hope you don't mind.'

'Not at all. I was just about to come back.'

Daisy opens her mouth to say something but then obviously thinks better of it.

Daniel smiles.' Right, well, I'm just going through the wines with Hugo and our options for after-lunch liqueurs. I'll get Hugo up to speed. We'll be in the bar if you need us, I want to show him the cellar, and get organised.'

I nod curtly. I need space. I need to organise myself, focus. I must concentrate on the food and not pay any attention to what's going on around me, not Daniel, not Daisy and certainly not Hugo.

As they leave the room, Daisy asks, 'So, what will I do first?'

'Get the potatoes and start peeling.'

I work backwards, thinking quickly; timing is everything.

If the first course is at one-thirty, the main course will be at two and dessert at three. I check the cooking times for each dish; steak is quick and easy, but I need to make peppercorn sauce, mushroom and cream sauce and a tamarind sauce for the chicken breasts. I also need a prawn cocktail sauce. Marie Rose is quick to make and tastes better with malt whisky, and I make a mental note to ask Daisy to get the alcohol from Hugo.

Daisy is prepping the potatoes for small roasties with rosemary, garlic and thyme. I'll also triple cook chips.

'After that, Daisy, please peel the apples.'

I scan my notes and make a mental note of the quantities of apples for the pies. I'll make extra, I always do just in case there's a disaster and besides, Daniel can always serve it tomorrow in the bar.

'This is fun, isn't it?' Daisy smiles, chopping the potatoes; she measures the length of them, side by side, so the chips will be all the same length. 'Ah, here's Billy. Hello Billy.'

Billy, the sous-chef, appears at ten. He strolls inside looking unsure, grumpy and resentful.

'Hi, I'm Ronda.' I smile, but he doesn't respond.

While I wait for him to take off his coat and put on his apron, I unwrap my eight-piece leather roll of kitchen knives.

'Oh, gosh!' Daisy exclaims. 'Are they your knives? They look amazing.'

'They're Japanese,' I explain. 'Crafted from Japanese Damascus stainless steel.' I don't add that they have an official Rockwell hardness rating of 60+/- 2 with 1% carbon for surgical sharpness and strong G10 handles. They're small details but essential to me.

'I've read that all good chefs have their own knives. What are they all for?'

I point them out, in size order, proud of the present Tina gave me after I graduated from the army and began my career as a chef and before I appeared on TV.

'This is a paring knife, this a utility, small and large santoku, small and large chef's and a bread and carving knife.'

'Bet they cost a lot.' Billy stands beside us, tying his apron.

'They were a gift,' I reply, knowing they cost almost a thousand pounds.

'So, I guess you're in charge today. What do you want me to do?'

'You can fillet the chicken and then clean the prawns.'

He doesn't say much, but I watch him as we all go about our business. He's as economical with his words as he is with his actions. He knows what he's doing. What he does, he does well.

Hugo pops in and out of the kitchen, and it's Daisy who tries to strike up a conversation with him each time. She asks him multiple questions.

I love your accent, where are you from? Paris, he replies. Where do you live? London. Do you like drinking wine? Yes. Have you ever met anyone famous? Only Ronda.

31

I look up and he winks. I look away.

Suddenly I'm transported back to last August when I was employed to cater for Herr Schiltz at Castle Calder. It was his second wife's fiftieth birthday but, unknown to the guests, Inspector Joachin from Europol had asked me to be his '*eyes and ears*'. It wasn't until after the weekend Hugo told me he was an undercover European police officer.

'Well, I've met someone more famous than Ronda,' Daisy announces, swinging her shoulders excitedly.

'There's no one more famous than Ronda,' Hugo replies good-naturedly.

'Well, last week we had that footballer here – the one from Liverpool. What's his name, Billy? You know, who was the guy from the famous football team?'

'Len Musgrove,' Billy adds, 'Arsenal.'

'Wow!' Hugo looks impressed.

I remember he said how he sometimes works privately for functions or well-known Michelin restaurants in France and I wonder in what capacity he's here today. He has the same laid-back and easy countenance, and he teases Daisy playfully. He's good-natured and funny and I listen to their banter.

What is Hugo doing *here*?

'Len was lovely. He even let me take a selfie.'

'I hope he realises how lucky he is to get a photo of you, Daisy.'

Daisy stops peeling potatoes to get her phone out from under her apron. She scrolls through the images on the phone while Hugo looks over her shoulder. I'd forgotten how long his eyelashes are.

'You've got some fascinating people on there,' he exclaims.

'Yeah, it's what I do. I like taking pictures. I want to

be famous one day. Sometimes the journalists come from celebrity magazines, like *Hello!* magazine, because we get lots of famous people here, don't we, Billy?'

'Yes.'

I glance up and Hugo meets my stare.

I return my attention to rolling the pastry for the apple pies.

'Look, there's Stefan, you know from that reality show? He's a real tool,' she giggles. 'Then this is Katie Price, she came here for dinner last week with her boyfriend, then Orlando Bloom came, his dad lives in Canterbury. And, this is ...'

I'm suddenly distracted. In the distance, there's a whirling sound, coming closer. Too loud for a lawnmower. Then there's the sound of a car engine, driving fast outside the kitchen window and the skid of car brakes on the gravel.

Daisy looks up.

'That's them! They're arriving,' she announces excitedly.

'It's deafening,' says Hugo, looking out of the window into the sky.

'That's the helicopter.' Daisy stands beside him. 'You won't see it from here. It lands on the field at the back. You can only see it from the dining room.'

'Helicopter?' Hugo and I say in unison.

'Yeah, there's plenty of room. Daniel knows the farmer. It comes here all the time with different guests. Last time it came here, I thought it was Madonna, but then it turned out to be some politician who I didn't know. But I wonder who it is today.' Her eyes gleam with excitement and she puts a hand to her unruly curls. 'I wonder who's coming.'

She runs across the hallway into the dining room, leaving the doors ajar.

The engine cuts off and the rotors slow down.

Daisy shouts, 'Oh. M. God. You're never going to believe it.' She covers her mouth with her hands.

'Who is it?' Hugo asks, moving quickly beside her.

I move to the door to watch.

'Oh my gosh!' Daisy continues, 'I just LOVE her.'

Billy continues to lay the filleted uncooked chicken in the dish. He seems unimpressed and stays focused on his task.

'Oh my God. It's is – it's her. I don't believe it. Look, she's getting out of the helicopter. Look!' Daisy's voice has reached a screaming pitch.

Daniel walks into the dining room.

'Our guest is here, Daisy. Shush.' He places his finger to his lips. 'Please. Go back to the kitchen. I know how excited you are, but not a word. Control your excitement. Be discreet.'

I return to my work station and lay out the pastry and roll it for the last time.

'But, do you know who that is?' she says and flounces back to the kitchen.

'Yes. Yes, I do. But discretion is important. Act like you're a young lady and you've seen it all before.'

Daniel takes a look around the kitchen and a deep breath as if he's controlling his nerves. 'Everything alright?' he asks me.

'Fine,' I reply, finding it hard not to stare at Hugo, who is standing beside him.

'Good. Don't worry. There's plenty of time. They're here early as there's a small presentation before lunch.'

Daniel straightens his tie. 'Right, I'll go and meet the guests.'

For the first time, I hear a quiver in his voice and his eyes look uncertain. I'm surprised, for a man who has been on television and regularly mixes with celebrities. What – or who – is suddenly making him so nervous?

After he's gone, Daisy returns to her place at the kitchen counter. She makes eye contact with me and hisses, 'It's Gloria— only the biggest singer in the whole world. What's she doing here?'

'Daisy. Enough. Please. Finish slicing the apples. They need to cook.'

* * *

I step up my speed in the kitchen, but I'm feeling more confident, knowing it's a small group and there's plenty of time. I spend a few minutes to make sure Billy is preparing the prawns by removing the head and veins that many people find disgusting.

Daisy finishes chopping small chunks of pineapple, and I begin to decorate the glass bowls for the starters with lettuce and diced tomatoes; I'll add the avocado nearer to serving time.

I'm mixing the Marie Rose sauce, adding a hint of malt whisky and cream when there's a commotion in the hallway. The guests are arriving and fleeting sounds of them greeting each other accompany my preparation; the slamming of car doors, footsteps on the gravel and Daniel's melodious welcoming voice in the hallway. Their voices recede, and I imagine them gathered in the cosy, warm security of the bar.

Daisy disappears and returns in two minutes. She whispers, 'Some of them are having coffee, but Gloria is drinking a martini cocktail. I just love her. She's so cool. Do you like her music?'

'Yes.' I continue to finish the apple pies. I've added a dash of cinnamon, and now I cover them with the light pastry.

'Did you add cinnamon?' Daisy asks.

35

'Yes.'

'I remember you did that on *Masterchef.*'

'Who else is here, Daisy?' Billy barely looks up.

'Nina King. She was on that reality TV show. She met that bloke from Essex, but it didn't last. She's so skinny.'

Billy nods. 'I like her. She's a stunner.'

'She's only gorgeous,' Daisy agrees. 'She's arrived in this red convertible with the roof down and music blaring and a matching scarf and hat. She's absolutely stunning.'

'I bet she's had a few jobs done.' Billy doesn't look up.

'No, she's all-natural.' Daisy frowns.

'Not those boobs.' Billy laughs. 'Or those lips. She's got a trout-pout like a fish.'

'No, she hasn't!'

Daisy doesn't realise Billy is winding her up.

'Billy, I need you to get the chicken in the oven, now.'

'Right, chef.'

'I wonder what they're all doing here.' Daisy leans on the counter.

'Daisy, please tidy the mess you've left.' I nod at the potato and apple skins.

'Yes, chef.' Daisy works as she talks. 'I know we're not supposed to ask anything, but I don't know who the other people are. I haven't seen them all.'

'Are they all here?' I ask, glancing at the clock.

Daisy shrugs. 'I couldn't see. One guy arrived on a motorbike – one of those flashy Goldwings. It looks amazing. I think he's foreign, maybe Spanish. He said '*hola*', isn't that Spanish?'

I tilt my head. Spanish?

Inspector Joachin is Spanish.

Is that the connection?

Is that why Hugo is here?

Daisy continues, 'There's a politician here too, Lord Someone-or-other, I've seen him on the telly, and a guy who looks the image of Idris Elba – he's American. He's really handsome, and I heard him tell Daniel he's parked his black Bugatti La Voiture at the front of the pub. Hugo has to drive it round to the back so no one will see it.'

As if on cue, Hugo walks in the back door bringing a gust of cold November air.

'Nice car?' Billy asks.

'Fantastic,' Hugo replies, smiling. 'I could get used to it.'

'Whose is it?'

'Aiden Moore's.'

'Get out of here.' Billy laughs.

'Who's he?' Daisy asks.

'Probably the youngest billionaire in the world – and a philanthropist.' Billy smiles. He finishes the prawns and washes his knife under the tap then something catches his eye, and he gazes out of the window. 'Well, if you think that's incredible, wait until you see this.'

Daisy rushes to the window.

Hugo looks over their shoulders, and I can't help myself. I move over to stand beside them, and I'm as close to Hugo as I was when we spied on the guests in Castle Calder. He's wearing the same seductive aftershave.

'It's a Lamborghini Veneno,' Billy says, appreciatively as if it's an Italian made ice-cream filling the sensations on his tongue.

'Wow!' Daisy whispers, 'Who's driving?'

'Try and sneak a look when he parks around the back, Daisy. The doors open upwards,' Billy replies.

'Who's driving it?' Daisy asks.

Billy shakes his head.

I have no idea, but it's Hugo who replies, 'That looks remarkably like Prince Abdul.'

'Get out of here.' Daisy bashes his arm playfully. 'A prince?'

'He's from the Middle East, and I believe he's the sultan's son.'

'What a medley of interesting characters,' I say pointedly to Hugo.

'Indeed.' But he doesn't look at me. He's already leaving the kitchen on his way to play the part of a perfect sommelier.

# 4

# Chapter 4

*'Guilt is just as powerful, but its influence is positive, while shame's is destructive. Shame erodes our courage and fuels disengagement.'*
**Brene Brown**

I'm preparing the tamarind sauce for the chicken, tasting and adding seasoning when Daisy announces, 'They're going through to the dining room for a presentation.'

'Are they all here?'

'Yes, the last man who arrived looks Indian, and he's got a driver with him.'

'Where's the driver now?' I ask, wondering if I need to cater for him.

Billy nods at the window. 'He's sitting outside in the Bentley. He looks a bit tough for a chauffeur. He's probably his bodyguard.'

Daniel appears. 'You've got fifteen minutes, Ronda. I've been assured it's a very short presentation – more of an introduction really.'

I nod.

Daniel disappears, and Billy stands at the fryer, checking the chips.

'I need the loo,' Daisy announces.

I'm not quick enough to stop her from disappearing, and I glance at Billy. He shrugs back at me as if to say, what can we do?

I fuss around, checking the order of the dishes, the final artistic details to add creativity to the plates. I need to make them look like my signature dishes.

Daisy is breathless when she returns.

'What's happening then?' Billy laughs. 'I bet you spied through the keyhole.'

'A blond guy is talking to them, but I didn't understand what he's saying.'

'Was it a foreign language?'

'No, it was about money and investments, so I glazed over.' Daisy grins at me. 'There's nothing more boring. I only want glamour. Gloria looks gorgeous. Do you think my hair would look nice, you know, straight and long like hers?'

\* \* \*

'Daisy, get the dishes for the starter from the fridge. I'll add the avocado.'

'Eight dishes.' Daisy grins with excitement, laying them on the counter. She slips her iPhone from her pocket and snaps a photograph of the prawn cocktail. 'It looks amazing, Ronda.'

'Now isn't the time, Daisy. Please put that away.'

'Yes, chef.'

'Ronda?' Daniel appears on the doorway. 'They've settled

down. Are you ready with the starter?'

'Yes.'

Daniel beams. 'We'll help you carry them in. Four of us, two plates each.'

Hugo appears behind him.

'Do they all have drinks?' he asks Hugo.

Hugo nods.

'Right,' I say. 'The starters are all the same. Daniel goes first, then Hugo, then Daisy and then me.'

The dining room is warm. The fire is glowing, and there's an expectant hush in the room as we file in with the plates of food. Daisy and I go clockwise, Hugo and Daniel go anticlockwise. I don't know anyone nor where they are sitting so I'm surprised to serve Gloria. Of course, I recognise her. I've read recently that the Canadian singer is currently on a European tour. Then a few weeks before Christmas, she's coming to London for the last five days of her concert in the O2. When I tried to get tickets, they were all sold.

Gloria looks at the dish I place in front of her, and she smiles sweetly at me. She's a few years younger than me and very glamorous. She wears a pretty red dress and matching chiffon scarf.

The second person I serve must be an Indian businessman. He's sitting beside Gloria, and he wears an expensive, Kiton K-50 grey checked suit worth over $50,000, and a pleasant smile.

'Thank you,' he whispers.

'You're welcome,' I reply softly.

I'm about to leave the room when suddenly Daniel takes my arm. He turns me gently to face the table, and I'm suddenly surprised to be the centre of attention. It's unexpected. All eyes on me except for one man, who sits with his back to me, I falter. My mouth dries, and my palms begin to perspire but then my army training kicks in. Confidence for life, and I appraise them quickly.

Aiden Moore, the handsome forty-year-old philanthropist, smiles confidently. Prince Abdul with sleepy eyes looks disinterested. The Indian businessman observes attentively, and I imagine he misses nothing. Gloria smiles like the star she is, and then I recognise Lord Michael Bonner, a disgraced peer involved in a scandal a few years ago but who refused to give up his seat in the House of Lords. Beside him is a ruggedly handsome man who I assume is the Spaniard who arrived by motorcycle. He leans to whisper something to Nina King. I vaguely recognise her from TV. She has long red hair, which falls in loose ringlets over her shoulders. She's a social media influencer who seems captivated by the Spaniard beside her. I can't see the face of the eighth person. The man with his back to me doesn't turn around.

'Today our chef is Ronda George. She may look familiar to you.'

Daniel uses his charming television voice and seductive smile.

'And, after sampling today's fare you won't be surprised to know she has trained in numerous Michelin-starred restaurants, won *Masterchef*, and now works privately for small groups such as this.' He pauses.

I hold my breath.

This endorsement from Daniel Clarkson is priceless. The best testimonial I could wish for. I turn to go back to the kitchen, but he holds me firmly around the waist.

'Ronda has come highly recommended.'

Gloria claps spontaneously, and it's only then that the blond man with his back to me turns around.

I should have known.

I should have recognised him, but his long curly blond hair is now cut into a trendy short quiff. His usual attire of worn jeans and hoodies has been replaced by a sharp grey suit and a pink shirt. His blue eyes crinkle in delight. He stands up to greet me. In front of everyone, he holds out his arms like we're old friends, reunited after years apart.

'Ronda, my darling.'

I stand rooted to the spot. My heart is filling with anger, my face turning to steel. He kisses me, just once on the cheek close to my mouth, before letting me go, then he addresses the table. His voice is clear and smooth, as if he's been taking classes from Daniel.

'I chose Ronda today, not only because of her amazing culinary skills but also because she's very discreet. She can keep a secret.'

His hand grips my arm in warning. I can't pull away without making a scene.

He faces me again, smiling. His eyes bore into mine as if to challenge me to defy his words.

I want to shout out that he's a lying, cheating, thief but I can't move. I want to take up my kickboxing stance and dropkick him in the stomach. I want to sit on top of him and beat his face to a pulp. A wave of savage anger takes possession of me, and my jaws clench as I tighten my fists at my side.

Then I'm distracted by a sudden movement. Hugo is at the back of the room. He moves forward.

I blink.

He carries a bottle of expensive wine, but he looks poised like

43

a panther ready, but ready for what?

Suddenly, the guests applaud, and it's Daniel who takes me gently by the arm and leads me from the dining room as if I'm a puppy going to the kennel.

Once I'm back in the safety of the kitchen, my eyes rest on my set of eight Japanese sharp kitchen knives. They are all clean and polished. Waiting.

* * *

Daniel pulls a piece of paper from his inside pocket and thrusts it into my hands.

'Here are the orders for the main course. You know the numbers, but these are the names, so you know in which order to serve the guests.'

He leaves the kitchen and disappears to the dining room.

'Are you alright?' Daisy asks. 'You look shocked, as if you've seen the devil himself.'

'I'm fine.' My hands are still shaking.

James is here. The thief.

How does he have the audacity to do this to me?

He's brazen.

'Ronda?' Billy asks, 'Are you sure you're okay? Hadn't we better get on?'

I can't speak. I don't know what to say. My ex, James Frampton, is sitting with celebrities, millionaires and philanthropists – all influential people – without a bother in the world. This cheap salesman is seated with a prince and a lord, and it seems as if he isn't a stranger to them. He is one of them. He's one of the guests accepted into this celebrity inner circle.

'Ronda?' Billy asks.

I look up. 'Yes, sorry.'

I click into military action, my training kicking in, and pushing my emotions aside I issue orders with precision, checking the list Daniel gave me.

Left to right from the front, clockwise.

*James Frampton – steak & mushroom sauce*

*Lord Bonner, on his left, steak and peppercorn & cream sauce*

*Enrique Suarez – steak – no sauce*

*Nina King – chicken*

*Aiden Moore – steak & mushroom sauce*

*Gloria – chicken*

*Prakash Khan – chicken*

*Prince Abdul – steak and peppercorn & cream sauce*

I bark out, 'Five steaks, two with pepper and cream sauce, two with mushroom sauce and one plain. Three chicken. Stir the tamarind sauce, Billy. Daisy, get the plates from under the hotplate.'

I turn away so that they can't see my hands shaking. I'm frightened to pick up a knife in case I go charging back into the dining room.

I could scalp James.

'Ronda?'

'What?'

'Who will clear the starter?' Daisy asks.

'Er, you and Daniel.'

'Will you serve the mains again?'

'I'll have to,' I mutter.

The kitchen door swings open.

'Everyone okay?' Hugo asks, but he's looking at me. I stare back at him, and our eyes meet across the room. He frowns.

His brown eyes look concerned.

Did he notice?

Does he know?

'We're fine.' I busy myself slicing the steak neatly into slices, placing them at an angle. 'Billy, how are the chips?'

'Good, chef.'

'Are the mushrooms ready?'

'Yes, chef.'

'Daisy, check the peas. I want the rosemary potatoes out of the oven.'

I don't look up. I'm conscious that Billy and Daisy work well together and we team up like a choreographed ballet moving effortlessly between each other. They respond quickly to my orders, and they are neat and clean. Each time I use one of my knives, I wash it carefully, dry it with a towel and replace it in the leather roll, so it's ready and clean for the next time.

The next time – I just hope James isn't around. Or maybe I should hope he is.

'Ready, chef.' Billy is at my elbow.

Daisy disappears to help Daniel to clear the starter while I add the decorative finishing touches to the dishes; a sprig of rosemary for the chicken, peppercorns for decorating the steak, small jugs of creamy mushroom sauce on the side, and roasted tomatoes on the vine.

'It looks delicious,' Daniel says, placing the dirty dishes near the sink. 'It's all in the presentation, Ronda.'

'She's amazing, isn't she?' Daisy whispers, looking over his shoulder. 'A real professional.'

She reaches into her pocket for her iPhone, but I frown.

She grins.

I wipe the edges of the plates with the cloth hanging from

my waistband.

I look at the plates lined up and ready to go.

'Right. Ready?'

'Are you?' Daniel looks at me, and I'm not quite sure what he means, but I ignore him. I file away his comment and his tone to mull over later on.

'Do you want to serve James?' Daniel asks me.

Hugo walks in. 'What can I do?'

'Let's do what we did the last time.' I nod at the plates. 'Hugo, you take the steak clockwise from the left, and you, Daisy, follow him. Daniel, you take the chicken for the two ladies. I have chicken for the Prakash Khan and Prince Abdul.'

The conversation stops as we enter the room, and there are murmurs of appreciation, but I don't hang around. I don't make eye contact.

Gloria exclaims her delight and Enrique mutters a compliment in Spanish. '*Gracias*, Ronda,' he adds, '*Que bueno.*'

We are in and out of the dining room quickly. I just want to get back to the kitchen, but I notice Hugo stays behind. As I leave the dining room, he's already at the bar and has picked up a chilled bottle of Chablis. It dawns on me that he's in the perfect position to listen to everything. He would have listened to the presentation. He knows what's going on.

Daniel follows me.

'Are you alright, Ronda?'

'I'm fine.'

'It's just that you seemed shocked, are you?'

I don't reply. I glance at the notepaper telling me the dessert orders but knowing I have plenty of time. It's a ploy to keep Daniel away, but he stands stubbornly at my side.

'Didn't you guess James was going to be here?' he insists.

47

I look up. 'No. I had no idea.'

'But, he recommended you. I told you. ' Daniel looks as if it's the most natural thing in the world.

'I know, but I assumed that it was ...' I'm lost for words, so I say, 'a secret lunch. I never expected James to be so well connected.'

Daniel throws his head back and laughs. 'Oh well, that explains it all. He actually said to me that you were still holding a candle for him.'

'He what?'

Daniel warms to his themes. 'James warned me that you would be shocked, but I didn't believe him. It's alright, Ronda. He confided in me. He says that you had a thing for him a while back, and that it didn't work out, but that he respected you.'

I stare at Daniel, knowing that he's been fed a lie.

Another lie by James. I want to correct him. I want to tell him that James is a good-for-nothing scumbag, but then it dawns on me. Daniel isn't going to believe me when it's James who is sitting amongst not only celebrities but also royalty and probably, more importantly, people of influence.

'If it's any consolation, Ronda.' Daniel smiles at me. 'Unfortunately for me, I think he's still holding a candle for you.'

* * *

While they are eating their main course, I decide it's a good time to use the bathroom. I close the door of the toilet cubicle, lock it and fish out my iPhone from my tunic pocket.

I text Tina.

*James is here.*

I wait, but she doesn't respond. She may have a business

lunch. I type.

*He's acting like I'm still in love with him. Daniel guesses that there's something between us and he says James still holds a candle for me.*

No reply.

I check down my list of contact phone numbers and stop at Inspector Joachin. My finger hovers over the buttons, and then I type quickly.

*What the hell is Hugo doing here in Kent?*

But then I change my mind. I don't want to be involved. I delete the text and close my phone.

I flush the toilet. Wash my hands, and as I leave the bathroom, someone in the dark hallway is behind me. A hand grabs my wrist and pulls me along. 'Ronda, come with me quickly,' James hisses.

He leads me away from the dining room toward the empty bar, past the rows of bottles and shining glasses and the special romantic nooks to a recess where steps are leading upstairs which I assume is to Daniel's flat.

He pushes me against the wall.

'Don't think about saying anything.' He grabs me by the throat. He's never been violent before. 'Say anything about the money, and you're dead.' Then he smiles, his charming smile which now looks wolf-like and insincere. 'You can see, I know a lot of important people, and you will be nothing, *nothing*,' he hisses, 'If you breathe a word to anyone.'

'What about my savings?' I choke.

'I'll give you your poxy bit of money. I'll give it to you in a couple of weeks, but meantime keep quiet. Do you understand?'

I'm surprised at his tight grip, and I consider kneeing him

where it hurts and beating him to a pulp, but I want my money.

I nod.

He releases me.

'Good,' he whispers. 'Now we know where we both stand.'

Then he's gone. It's all over so quickly, and the only testament I have that it happened is my sore neck. I take off my bandana, ruffle my hair and take a deep breath before refastening it around my head.

Why was I so slow?

I kickbox so why didn't I fight back?

Fight or flight – I stood like an idiot when I could have flattened him on the floor in seconds. Why didn't my instinct kick in – my self-preservation? All my army training. Confidence for life.

I've lost my edge.

Back in the kitchen, a stranger is standing in the doorway. He's broad-shouldered and well-dressed in an expensive dark suit.

'He wants to use the bathroom,' Billy whispers in my ear. 'He is Prakesh's chauffeur. I'll show him where it is, okay?'

I move aside, and as they pass me, I'm conscious of the man's presence, menacing yet somehow reassuring, depending on whose side you're on.

When they are out of earshot, Daisy whispers, 'I think that's Prince Abdul's chauffeur. He's been sitting in that car outside.'

'The Bentley belongs to Prakash Khan,' I say.

'Well, there's someone still in the car,' Daisy replies. 'There's two of them. They've both been wandering around outside.'

Billy reappears and joins our conversation. 'He's been having a good look around inside now.'

'The other driver hasn't moved. He came with Lord Bonner. He was on his phone, but now I think he's fallen asleep.' Daisy peers out of the window,

'Who is Prakash Khan, anyway?' Billy asks.

'I Googled him,' Daisy replies, turning from the window. 'He's in finance – he's an entrepreneur. Presumably, he does things like outsourcing.'

'What, like Indian call centres?' Billy asks.

'And he's an accountant.' Daisy looks pleased to be able to share the information. 'He seems very clever and very, very wealthy.'

The door swings open, and Prakash's bodyguard reappears.

'Would you like something to eat?' I ask him.

He shakes his head and smiles. 'No, thank you.' His voice is as dark as his eyes. 'I'll wait outside.'

We watch him go and, as Billy turns away, Daisy leans closer to me.

'He carries a gun. It's strapped to his chest, under his arm on the left.'

I smile; I had noticed. My army training has kicked in. The man is more than a chauffeur.

'I bet he's a bodyguard,' Daisy says.

'I think you could be right.' Troubled, I turn away. I need to think.

How has James got involved with these high flyers?

When I knew him nine months ago, he was knocking on doors. Now he's suddenly at the top, playing dice with the rich and famous. How has he managed to do that? Meanwhile, the other half of my brain is roaring inside saying, it doesn't matter how or why he's done it. At least I now finally stand a chance of getting my money back.

# 5

# Chapter 5

*'My music comes from many, many, many places. My emotions, my feelings, my thoughts, and conversations I have with people I know who influence me.'*
**Alicia Keys**

My head is full of noise.

I want to shout at the arguing voices. I don't care that James is dining with these people of influence. I want nothing to do with him. I want my money. The thirty thousand pounds he stole from me—all my savings. I was going to invest in a restaurant on the south-east coast of England; he took my money and my dreams. He's a thief. How can I trust what he says now? Why does he even want me here?

I check the dessert list in my hands then toss it on the counter.

'Daisy, take the pies out. They're ready, and they can cool a little. Billy, I made an apple crumble as an extra this morning, and ...' I check my list. 'Gloria and Nina prefer apple crumble. We'll need to put the vanilla ice cream in the small dishes and use the small pouring jugs for the home-made Baileys.'

'That's one of your signature dishes, isn't it?' Daisy smiles.

I nod. I busy myself with the task of arranging the plates and dishes. Instinct, my military training and my discipline take over. I'm working on automatic pilot. When you've cooked buffets and banquets in some of the world's hotspots, and catered for majors and generals in the army, this lunch is a doddle. There's no threat of enemy fire, no dodging bullets, no casualties, no deaths. Not yet.

James.

He may be a casualty.

I need to get him alone and next time on my terms. He's not going to threaten me.

'Did you see Gloria?' Daisy swoons and then fakes a Canadian accent. 'Gloria's from Montreal. Could I get my hair cut like hers? With bangs – that's what they call a fringe in Canada – like hers?'

'Your hair is too frizzy,' replies Billy. 'Her hair is sleek and golden. A fringe wouldn't suit you.'

'Do you think I could get a photo, a selfie? What if I bump into her in the bathroom?'

'No.' Billy pushes her aside. 'Daniel would go mad. He said no photos.'

Daisy makes a remark, but I don't hear it, and Billy ignores her.

'What do you think they're all doing?' Daisy asks, and when we don't reply, she says, 'I bet it's something exciting like a new album, or video or something.'

'I thought you said it was about investment?' I say.

'Well, that is an investment, isn't it?' Daisy replies curtly. 'You need to put money into music, and there's a lot of them here to do that.'

'Why do you say that?' asks Billy.

'Well, there's a lot of money around that table, investors and people with influence. I bet they're doing a music or video deal.'

'There's no record label manager, is there?' Billy asks.

'No.'

'There are no music producers, either?' Billy insists.

Daisy shrugs. 'I don't know who they all are.'

Billy reaches out and swivels around my discarded dessert list to read it better. He squints at the names beside the desserts.

'Look, Lord Bonner, he's a politician. Enrique Suarez is the bloke on the motorbike. Nina King, we know is a reality star and blogger. Aiden Moore, who looks like Idris Elba, has lots of money – he's a billionaire, Gloria is possibly the best-selling singer of all time, bigger than Lady Gaga and Kylie and—'

'Daisy, check there are small spoons for the ice cream,' I say.

'Yes, all okay.'

Billy continues, 'Prakesh Khan who has the bodyguard outside. Prince Abdul who looks miserable—'

'And, lastly the good-looking guy, James.' Daisy looks at me. 'Do you know him, Ronda?'

'Vaguely,' I say.

'He obviously likes you.'

I shake my head, and the heat in the kitchen makes me feel suddenly hot.

'Are you blushing?' Daisy asks with a giggle.

'He's not my type,' I lie, tidying up the dishes, cleaning the edges with a cloth. 'Right, let's get ready. You'll need to collect the mains. Have they finished eating?'

Daisy ignores me. 'Gosh, how could you not fancy James? He's gorgeous, and besides, he's the one to know. He's the interesting one – apart from Gloria, of course.'

'What do you mean?' I look up.

Daisy's eyes are sparkling with mischief. 'I heard him speaking. He's the one in charge. He's the one who's put together this whole thing. He's arranged this meeting, and he did the opening presentation.'

My mouth falls open, then I close it quickly.

'He's the one,' Daisy continues, 'that has a business proposition for them all. He called it a worthwhile venture that will quadruple all of their wealth.'

* * *

Daniel calls Daisy to help him clear the table.

'This is the side I don't like,' Billy says when we are alone in the kitchen. 'The part of the job that stinks.'

'What do you mean?' I ask.

Billy nods at the door to the dining room. 'Cooking for the likes of them. Those posh nobs – give me the regulars any day, some of the locals were well fed up with Daniel closing the pub today.'

'Really?'

'Yes, and it's not right. They're not stupid. Daniel thinks he can get away with it, but the regulars want loyalty. They don't want these sort of people flying in here from London; or wherever it is they come from, in their expensive cars and helicopters. This is their home. They hate it when the celebrity magazines fall over themselves to get a scoop about the next person walking through the door. It's so staged. Daniel tips off the reporters and the celebs know it, they love it. But think of the regulars, the people who live in the village. It's their local pub and I think Daniel's made a huge mistake.'

'Does he do it often?'

Billy shakes his head. 'It's the first time he's actually closed the whole pub. Normally, folk turn up for a meal and want a bit of privacy, and we cater for them privately in the dining room, but to actually close the pub, it's ridiculous. It's not fair. It's—'

Daniel and Daisy appear through the swing doors carrying the plates.

'That was a success.' Daniel beams at me.

'Who didn't eat the steak?' I ask glancing at one of the plates of hardly touched food.

'That was Prince Abdul, but don't worry. You know what princes are like ...'

I don't, but I stay quiet. I attend to the dessert, adding a sprig of fresh mint to the apple pie for decoration and a cinnamon stick on the edge of the vanilla ice cream bowls, followed by home-made Maltesers to accompany the Baileys.

'Service,' I call.

'Same as last time?' asks Daisy.

'Yes, please.'

Hugo arrives.

We pick up the dishes and carry them through to the dining room. The window is now open, and Prince Abdul stands beside it, smoking a cheroot. His thoughtful eyes follow Hugo around the room.

Back in the kitchen, Billy is waiting for me.

'Can I go outside for a smoke?'

'Yes, as long as no one sees you.'

After he's gone, Daisy rolls up her sleeves and runs the plates under the hot tap before placing them in the dishwasher. I help her. I carry the pots and pans to the sink.

'Will I be able to go soon?' she asks.

'I guess so, once this is done.'

She nods.

'Do you think I could get some photos?'

'Daniel said no.'

'What Daniel doesn't see ...'

'Didn't you sign a non-disclosure agreement?'

'Yes, so?'

'So, they could sue you.'

'They could try. I haven't any money.' She grins.

'You might go to prison.'

'Really?'

I shake my head. 'I don't know, but you must be careful, Daisy. It's all about trust.'

I put the saucepans and pots from the main course and dessert near, and set out fresh dessert bowls in case anyone wants more.

I pick up a tea towel and stand beside her.' What do you think James's proposition is all about then?'

She smiles, impressed that I've picked up a tea towel to help her.

'I couldn't hear them properly, Ronda, but it sounded as if he gave an introduction as if he's selling something that he wants them to invest in. I heard him talking about a sort of computer thingy.'

'Who, James?'

'Yes, it's like he was really enthusiastic, and he asked anyone if there were any questions.'

'And were there any?'

'Enrique wanted to know more and Nina was keen. James

promised a proper presentation with figures and more details—
'

'Daisy!' Daniel calls from the doorway. 'I hope you're not gossiping.'

We both turn around.

'No, I wasn't.'

'Good! You know the rules, and if you can't stick to them, you'll have to go.'

'I'm washing up,' she wails.

'She wasn't indiscreet,' I say. I take a chance that he didn't hear our whole conversation. 'She was hoping to get a photograph with Gloria – a selfie.'

'That's out of the question. Now, they'll want tea and coffee shortly. Mint tea for Prince Abdul, Earl Grey for the ladies, and fruit tea for Enrique. The others are having coffee.' He heads to the percolator. 'Where's Billy?'

'I think he's in the toilet,' I reply.

'I hope he's not outside having a cigarette.'

\* \* \*

When Billy returns from outside, he sets up the coffee and organises the tea.

'It's easy for me to do, Ronda. I know where everything is. Do you want one?'

'What's the protocol for the staff to eat?' I ask. 'Do you want me to make you something?'

Billy looks surprised. 'Don't worry about us, we're fine. It's different if we're here all day, but you go ahead, you have to drive back to London later on.'

'I won't go just yet.'

I'm conscious of the vast sum of money Daniel is paying me. Half of which has been paid to my account and the second half that will be transferred tomorrow morning. It's more than I could have anticipated. Besides, I haven't given up hope of speaking to James on my own. Now that I know he's here, I'm ready for him. My hands rest on my Japanese kitchen knives.

'Ronda?' Hugo says from the doorway.

I look up.

'Don't disappear on me, will you.'

'Why?'

'I'd like a word with you after the guests have gone.'

'Are they going now?' Daisy turns from the sink, and Hugo laughs.

'No, not yet, they're finishing coffee.'

'And cocktails?' she asks. 'Is Gloria having another martini?'

'Not at the moment,' Hugo says with a smile, and he winks at me. 'I'll see you later.'

Daisy sighs and after he's gone she says, 'I think he likes you.'

'You have a very fanciful imagination.'

But at the same time, I wish my heart didn't do excited flips when Hugo was around.

'By the way, thanks for not informing on me. Daniel's got a real temper. It's alright when things go his way, but when he loses it, my goodness, you don't want to be around him.'

'Does he lose it often?'

'He used to when Jenny was here.'

'His wife? Did you know her?'

'Yes, she used to run this place. Jenny's lovely. She moved to the south coast last year. She said she couldn't stand him anymore. She said if she'd stayed any longer, she'd probably end up killing him.'

'I'm sure that was just a figure of speech.'

Daisy shakes her head, knowingly. 'You wouldn't say that if you'd heard them argue.'

* * *

I'm in the kitchen, at the small table, sipping coffee. There's a lull after lunch, and I'm waiting to see if anyone wants more to eat.

'I need to help Hugo,' Billy says, coming into the kitchen from the hallway. 'Daniel has to make a phone call, and he's asked me to show Hugo where the special liqueurs are in the cellar. He also wants the wine replaced, ticked and checked off, so nothing goes missing.'

'Is it an exceptional wine?'

I think of James ordering the best of everything. He did that in Paris with me once. He'd forgotten to bring his credit card, but he'd made good use of mine, including buying us matching engagement rings in a street off the Champs-Elysées.

Billy grins. 'You wouldn't believe how expensive it is.'

'Oh, I think I would.'

He disappears, and Daisy says she needs to go to the bathroom.

'You should wait until the guests leave, Daisy.'

'I can't, Ronda. I'm desperate.' She crosses her legs in mock desperation.

'Daniel won't be pleased if he catches you.'

'He won't be pleased if I wet my knickers either.'

I laugh. I guess this is her opportunity to see if she can meet Gloria and get a selfie. I decide that I'm not responsible for her. She will pay the price if Daniel catches her and if she's prepared to take the risk then who am I to stop her?

I sip my coffee thoughtfully.

Some of the guests are still sitting around the dining table, and a few have ventured into the bar. Occasionally, through the open door, I hear Aiden Moore's deep laugh and Lord Bonner's high pitched raised voice as if he's in the House of Lords. I remember caricatures in the newspapers at the time of his scandal, portrayed with revolting nasal hair and a pointed chin. When he was an MP he had lobbied for a rail line in the north of England that would have benefitted one of his investments. But he'd failed to include it on the register of MPs' interests. The business park he'd invested in would have profited hugely had the rail link been granted.

As an MP, Lord Bonner a property investor, had almost secured a government pledge of £60 million. It was only after due diligence by a local reporter and a junior minister that the secrecy on these rulings had been lifted. It had been deemed that it was 'in the public interest' to know who the investors were, and Lord Bonner had been in denial. He said he'd been unaware of the non-disclosure requirements. It was corruption at the highest level, and I had never liked him. Worse still. He had been in favour of the war in Afghanistan. He knew nothing. Nor did he care.

I close my eyes, remembering my experience after my mother died. My father, Brigadier Charles George, insisted I sign up as an officer with the British Army at Sandhurst. I learned leadership skills, but it was more than that. It taught me how to evaluate situations, and what people say and how they say it. It taught me how to respond with a measured response, damage limitation, in a conflict area. Peacekeepers, army, defenders, attackers, all skills with different strengths. I had thought I might have lost these skills in the three years of being a civilian, but upon seeing James today, an inner strength has taken over. An inner core of determination that surprises me. And, more importantly, patience. It's not who wins the battle but who wins the war. This was mine to win.

Last February 14th, James had left me standing in the registry office with Tina and two of my best army friends at my side. He'd said we should have a quiet wedding, unassuming and romantic. He said he would bring the best man and his mother. That morning we'd waited, and waited and when he didn't show, I'd assumed he'd had an accident. Frightened, full of dread and dark images, my first thought was to ring the police, but when I reached for my mobile, there was a message.

*Sorry, Hun. Can't do this—cold feet. I will always love you. James* x

I was baffled, hurt, angry, shocked, sad, humiliated, but then I remembered how he'd taken all my money. He'd said it was for our future. He wanted to invest in his technology-based company that would make us millions and I'd believed him. I had allowed him to take my savings, the money I'd put aside for a little restaurant on the coast. I had trusted him.

We were engaged. We were getting married, but then all I had left was this pathetic text message.

I'd tried to call him, but he didn't reply. I went to everywhere we'd been together; bars, restaurants and all the places where he once lived before moving in with me. I even went to his mother's house in Suffolk. But she said he was safe. There was absolutely nothing for me to worry about and that sometimes relationships didn't work out. She was frail. He was never close to her but she still defended him. But when I searched further for him, no one knew where he was. He'd fallen off the radar. It dawned on me then that he had very few friends and he'd spent most of his time on his computer. He had geek friends or people he'd known or spoken about on the Internet, but I hadn't taken much notice. They had only been vague references. He had been very secretive about everything.

I sigh. Now I don't care about any of that. I don't care about James. People only ever have one chance with me, and he'd had it. All I want now is my money.

'Ronda?'

I look up.

'The guests are going, would you like to say goodbye to them?' Daniel smiles.

I don't.

I don't want to see any of them – except James, who I want to hang upside down and shake like a money tree before I cut out his innards.

When I venture into the bar, Lord Bonner's face is flushed and he's nursing a large brandy. He ignores me. But Aiden Moore rises to his feet and shakes my hand. His voice is deep, his hands gentle and his smile broad. He could easily be a movie star.

'Thank you, Ronda. That was delicious. Next time I'm in London, I'll ask you to cook for me.'

I smile. 'That would be my pleasure.'

'You're coming back next week, remember?' James stands up. His eyes are sparkling as if he's excited. 'Well, I hope you are, Aiden?'

Aiden nods. 'I'll give it some thought.'

I turn away, distracted by a roaring sound outside. I glance to the window where Gloria's helicopter is stirring; the propellers are swirling, and it rises with a wobble into the air

In the far corner of the bar, Nina King and Prince Abdul are deep in conversation, and then Enrique Suarez appears at the far end of the room holding his motorcycle helmet looking like a hero from an action movie.

'Thank you, Ronda. I hope to see you again.' He speaks perfect English but with an accent. He shakes my hand, then turns his attention to the group and announces, 'I'm leaving now.'

That's my cue to leave the bar, and I return to the kitchen.

Daisy is alone, staring at her phone.

'Quick, Ronda. Look!' she whispers, holding out her iPhone. 'I got a picture of Gloria but no selfie.'

She scrolls through the images.

Daisy got more than one picture. There's one of Gloria with Nina King in the bar, and there are also a couple of images of Prince Abdul with Lord Bonner, Prakash Khan in deep conversation with Enrique Suarez and another of Aiden Moore with Daniel. And lastly, a couple of images of Gloria outside near the helicopter kissing James goodbye.

'Aiden Moore is gorgeous, and he's so lovely.'

'Can you AirDrop them to me?' I pull out my iPhone.

'I didn't think you were one for photos?'

I grin. 'I'm more like you than you think.'

My phone pings when the seven photos arrive on my phone and I pocket it quickly.

'We'd better hide our phones,' I say. 'Daniel won't be pleased.'

'He won't know.' She grins but pockets her iPhone. 'It's been great working with you, Ronda.'

'Come on, Daisy. Help me tidy up, and then you can go home.'

Between us, we finish cleaning up the kitchen.

Hugo pops his head around the door. 'The dining table is empty if you want to clear?'

Daisy occasionally disappears to collect the dirty glasses, and I can only assume that Hugo doesn't want to miss out on eavesdropping on the conversations in the bar.

Ten minutes later, all the guest have gone. I listen to the engines roaring along the gravel to the main road. I check my watch. It's three-thirty.

Daniel appears, looking happy. 'That was very successful, Ronda. Thank you.'

'No problem.' I smile.

'In fact, it was so successful; they'd like you back again. Can you make it next Wednesday, same times, same conditions?'

'A different menu?' I grin.

Daniel smiles. 'I'll check with James.'

'Has he left?'

'Yes, he was in a hurry. He left with Lord Bonner. He said to say goodbye.'

I turn away. The elusive Pimpernel has avoided me again, and I feel the rising anger boiling and bubbling inside me, and it continues on my solitary car journey back to London.

6

# Chapter 6

*'It takes tremendous discipline to control the influence, the power
you have over other people's lives.'*
**Clint Eastwood**

I've walked Molly in the dark, made supper and I'm sitting
down in my flat to a small chicken stir fry when the phone
rings.

'It's Hugo,' he says.

'What do you want?'

'You left before I had a chance to speak to you.'

'Why do you want to speak to me?' I fork a mouthful of
vegetables into my mouth.

Molly sits at my feet watching, making sure I'm not going to
get up and leave her suddenly.

'I didn't know you knew James Frampton.'

'So?'

'So, how do you know him?'

'Tell me something first, were you there today because
you're a sommelier or because of Inspector Joachin and your

job as a policeman for Europol?'

'Are you still mad at me?'

'I want to know.'

'Joachin wanted you to work with us, Ronda. Why did you say no?'

I pause, thinking.

Inspector Joachin wanted me to work with them – *not* Hugo – my instinct was right. Hugo has given me no thought at all. Hugo is a player.

He continues speaking in my ear. 'It would have been great to work with you again, Ronda.'

Slightly mollified, I continue eating, waiting for him to speak more.

'Did I upset you in Scotland?' he asks.

Did he what? He only kissed me as if he meant it, and like no one has kissed me before. Then I realised it was all a cover-up, so we weren't caught spying.

I want to scream; *you used me.*

'Ronda? Are you there?'

'Yes.'

'Well?'

'No, you didn't upset me.'

*It was your duty*; I add silently. That's what he'd told me. It was your duty not to get caught and to take advantage of me, and I certainly wasn't going to put myself in that situation again.

'Inspector Joachim was really impressed with you. You have all the right instincts and attributes to work with us, Ronda.'

'You mean, I trained in the military for ten years.'

'Yes, but you're also smart, discreet and, if I may say so – an excellent chef.'

I lift my wine glass, and Molly looks up.

Hugo is charming. I'll give him that.

'Would you have dinner with me?' he asks.

I spit out my wine.

'What?' He laughs. 'You sound surprised.'

I wipe the spilt wine off my chin.

'No, no dinner.' I'm not getting involved with him. I'm not letting him think he can seduce me, or get what he wants so easily.

'Coffee then?' he asks.

I look at Molly. Her chin is resting on her front paws and she's watching me with her big, brown eyes as if she has the answer.

'Do you like dogs?' I reply.

\* \* \*

The park is deserted. It's a bright but damp November morning, and the trees are holding on to the few leaves they have left, reminding me of my summer of dog walks, my angst and soul searching. So many times I'd walked through these woods, stomping, shouting aloud, furious with myself that I had been so foolish as to trust James.

I have bared my soul to Molly and Tina, almost to the point that they are both probably sick of me, and now, as I watch Hugo walk toward me, I know I must be careful. I wasn't going to let him knock down my defences so easily.

'Hi, Ronda.' He kisses me on both cheeks and then bends down to pet Molly.

To my utter dismay, she licks his hands then rolls on her back in submission for a tummy tickle. She loves him already.

'She's a tart,' I say disgustedly, tugging on Molly's lead, annoyed at her obvious delight with Hugo. 'Come on; we'll get cold standing still. We can let her off the lead up here.'

We move away from the main gate and walk along the pathways and I let Molly loose. I pull an old tennis ball from my pocket and she jumps enthusiastically. When I throw it, she chases it in a long loping, excited run.

'So, Ronda. Where will we start?'

'Tell me why you were at The Cockerel and the Guinea Pig last Wednesday.'

I want Hugo to trust me. If he's there in a police capacity, although I'm not working with them, I need to know they trust me enough to confide in me.

'Enrique Suarez, thirty-three, is an author, journalist, marketing consultant, speaker and social media guru. He's been involved in a couple of dubious deals in Spain. He's the owner of an antiques business in Seville. It makes money, but quite frankly, we believe it's a front for another type of activity.'

'Why?'

'He purchased a valuable set of pearl earrings on the black market.'

'You set him up?'

Hugo smiles. 'Sort of, yes.'

'So what's it really about?'

Hugo pushes his hands deeper into his grey trench coat pocket and he watches Molly return with the ball and drop it at my feet. I throw it again.

'We didn't really know what was going on, and then we found out about the secret meeting that was taking place last Wednesday and Inspector Joachin thought it would be a good idea to have someone on the inside to see what's happening.'

'But you have no jurisdiction in England.'

'No, that's right. I was an observer. We weren't sure if Enrique was meeting someone to fence some goods or to buy other valuable, high-end market items on the black market. You know we investigate the disappearance of rare, cultural items and we thought he might lead us to a European hub – a gang of dealers that sell across borders to the Chinese or the Russians. We wanted to find out what's going on before we involve the appropriate police forces in Europe or beyond.'

'So you had no idea when you walked into the pub last Wednesday?'

'None.'

'And, did you find out?' I ask.

'Oh, yes. James Frampton did a whole introduction.'

I can't imagine James is interested in antiques or that he has contacts in the underworld, although now I'm beginning to wonder if I ever knew him at all. I don't react. I keep calm, throw the ball for Molly and I don't look at Hugo.

'And?'

'Well, it has nothing to do with buying and selling cultural artefacts.' Hugo frowns.

'So, it doesn't involve you?'

'It's about a new Internet currency called INTmon – short for international money, and James wants to get people on board to back his idea and invest in the scheme.'

'It's James's idea?'

'Presumably.'

'Is there a problem with that?' I bend down to pick up the ball, wishing I'd brought Molly's thrower. Hugo takes the ball from my hand and hurls it much further than me. Molly chases it.

'Have you heard of Bitcoin?'

'Vaguely.'

'It's a decentralised digital currency. There's no central bank or particular administrator, and there's no need for intermediaries.'

'So who controls it? How does it work?'

'Network nodes verify transactions through cryptography and these are recorded in their own public distributed ledger called a blockchain. They are created as a reward for mining.'

'Mining?'

'Bitcoin mining is done by specialised computers. The job of the miner is to secure the network and to process every Bitcoin transaction.'

'How do they do that?'

'They solve a computational problem which allows them to chain together blocks of transactions. Which is the ledger called a blockchain.'

I look at him.

Molly has returned with her ball, so he picks it up and throws it. He smiles at me. His nose is red from the cold, but his dark eyes are soft and warm. We walk in silence and I digest the information.

'So, what happens next?' I ask.

I throw the ball, but Molly is off sniffing at some bushes.

'These bitcoins can be exchanged for other currencies and can be used to purchase other products and services—'

'All online?'

'Yes.'

'Don't Facebook and Amazon want their own currencies?'

'You're well informed, Ronda.'

'I read the news.'

'Well, Facebook aims to launch its own global currency and financial infrastructure, Libra. They are in talks with the Swiss banks, and they're also in talks with different merchants to accept payment in return for lower transaction fees, but we're digressing from James. Facebook is transparent, and it's up to the governments and the legal powers that be to see if they manage to achieve it. Many governments want to stop it. They want to be able to control the banks and finances. They don't want businesses to have global power.'

'So where does James come in?'

'He's more aligned to Ruja Ignatova, the Crypto Queen.'

I smile. 'Really? A crypto queen.'

As he talks, he throws Molly's ball each time she brings it back.

'Back in June 2016, Doctor Ruja Ignatova walked onto the stage at Wembley Arena wearing an expensive ball gown, long diamond earrings, and bright red lipstick. She had an audience of adoring fans, and she told them about her product, OneCoin. It was on course to become the world's biggest cryptocurrency. The people went mad – crazy – they were cheering for her. She managed to persuade them to invest billions but, in actual fact, it was a pyramid scheme. She's since disappeared. Now, she's either a very wealthy woman or she's lying dead somewhere. No one knows where she is. You see, the first thing you must know is that money only works when people trust it, or other people give it a value – and they trusted her. It's always been about trust. For years people have tried to create a form of digital money, independent of state-backed currencies, but they've failed – once they realise the person in charge could manipulate the supply and forgery was easy, they lost the trust.'

'And you think James is involved in this?'

'Let me finish, Ronda. The reason Bitcoin was so popular was that the Bitcoin owners had independent but identical copies, and this blockchain database recorded each transaction. This is important. Each transaction as it occurred would go simultaneously in everybody's books. It's all mathematical and to be honest, complicated. But, the bottom line is because of the blockchain, Bitcoins can't be faked, they can't be hacked or double-spent.'

Molly trots along beside us. She's tired, and her tongue is hanging out. I put the sloppy tennis ball in my pocket while I assimilate all the information.

'People all over the world invested in the Crypto Queen. British people spent almost thirty million euros, two million in a single week. In three years, more than four billion euros was invested in dozens of countries as far as Pakistan to Canada and Brazil to Norway. It was incredible. They believed in her.'

'So, I still don't understand the problem.'

'It turned out to be a massive scam. They didn't have a computer programmer to build a blockchain.'

'What?'

Hugo shakes his head. 'When she was questioned, it turns out they were only using a standard SQL Server database – which isn't suitable for a real cryptocurrency. By this time Doctor Raja had purchased multi-million-dollar properties including on the Black Sea, and she threw magnificent parties on a luxurious yacht. She even had pop stars performing for and endorsing her. Then one day, she vanished. The FBI traced her to Greece and then she disappeared off the radar – never to be seen again.'

'So, someone could have bumped her off?'

Hugo shrugs. 'Anything is possible. The bankers were certainly the people who might have done it. But there's no evidence. For a while, they thought someone might have kidnapped her, but no one came forward to demand a ransom.'

I stop in my tracks. 'But what does this have to do with James?'

'Well, the premise for selling the internet currency, as I said, was pyramid selling. Hundreds of innocent investors are encouraged to part with their money in a pyramid scheme on a global basis to eventually float the business on the stock exchange to make millions. The business is fronted by celebrities, influencers and enablers who are recruited to promote the scheme through social media.'

'You think James is developing a cryptocurrency?'

'After his introduction last week to the group of wealthy influencers, I don't think it, Ronda. We know what he's doing. And, he's about to perform the biggest scam the country has ever seen.'

\* \* \*

I'm sitting at the kitchen table in my flat with Tina. We have an empty wine bottle between us. Our dirty dishes are in the sink, but I'm not ready to tackle those just yet. I'm still getting my head around what Hugo told me.

'This is massive,' Tina says, shaking her head. 'This is probably international fraud at the highest level.'

'It will be if James gets the endorsement from the other seven people at lunch last Wednesday.'

'Pyramid schemes are notoriously dodgy.' Tina waves her glass in the air. 'Any more wine?'

I pull another bottle of Chardonnay from the fridge and unscrew the top.

'Why doesn't Inspector Joachin approach them all individually and tell them James is a fraud?'

'Hugo says they want to find out more. He reckons James isn't the brains behind it all. He's all bullshit and bluster. They want to catch the people at the top.'

'And Daniel wants you to go back next Wednesday and so does Hugo – well, Inspector Joachin?' She grins.

'Yes, and he's also asked me to find out what I can from James.'

'Did you tell Hugo he's your ex?'

'I had to. I told Hugo everything. I told him how James had bought tickets to Paris on my credit card and when we got there he proposed, but he'd left his wallet at home. Then how we were supposed to be getting married and James hadn't shown up, but he'd taken my fifty grand.'

'What did he say?'

I think back, trying to remember his reaction. He hadn't said much, but his dark eyes had clouded over.

'Nothing,' I reply. 'Hugo just listened. But I'd felt such a numpty. How could I have been so stupid?'

Tina ignores me. 'So, Hugo managed to get in as the sommelier to the private party.'

'I think Inspector Joachin knows everyone.'

Tina nods. 'But they didn't know what was going on?'

'Not at all, they were suspicious of Enrique, he's not as legit as he makes out, so when someone invited him to a secret lunch, Hugo wangled his way in. As the sommelier he was in the best position to watch everyone and listen to what was going on. It was quite a revelation to him. They're all so massively influential. He'd heard of Gloria and her music, of course, and he'd seen Nina on TV. Since then he's done his homework and all the others are very wealthy investors.'

'Typical male.' Tina snorts. 'Only interested in women.'

'He's not,' I say defensively and then realise Tina is laughing.' Stop!'

'I think you like Hugo.'

At the mention of Hugo's name Molly sits up.

'Look, even Molly likes Hugo,' Tina teases me.

Molly wags her tail.

'Have you no loyalty, Molly?' I ask her, but she lies down and regards me silently with her head on her paws.

Tina pushes her hair behind her ears. 'So, what will you do, Ronda?'

'Hugo wants me to contact James and find out what's going on, but I haven't got his new number. This is what James does. He makes out he knows everyone, even me, and then he takes off. I bet he sees these investors as cash cows.'

'Probably.'

'They're influencers,' I say. 'They're very powerful, and they are very persuasive.'

'So, did he come up with this business plan?' she asks.

'He must be in it with someone else.'

'Could he write a software programme – a blockchain?'

'I don't know. James was always into computer technology, but I doubt he'd be able to do anything so complex. He wasn't particularly brilliant mathematically, as far as I can remember, only in the sense that he knew how to take my money.'

'Then it makes sense, if he's a charmer and a talker and he persuades all these people to invest, they're influencers, aren't they? Let's see the list again.'

I push it in front of her, and she reads my scruffy handwriting while I pull out my iPhone and scroll through the images that Daisy sent me. We compare the faces to my list.

1. UK – James Frampton – software developer.

2. US – Billionaire/investor/philanthropist – Aiden Moore

3. Middle East – Sultan's son – Prince Abdul

4. Canadian – Gloria – Top female celebrity/singer/billionaire/influencer/blogger.

5. Spanish – Enrique Suárez – author, journalist, marketing consultant, speaker & social media guru – influencer.

6. French – Nina King – reality TV star, social media and influencer.

7. UK – politician – public schoolboy, investor, Lord Michael Bonner

8. Indian – Prakash Khan – Brains to make it work – Accountant, banker and entrepreneur – outsourcing

'They're from all over the world,' Tina says.

'Apart from China and Japan, although Gloria has influence over there. All her concerts were a massive sell-out earlier in the year – just like at the O2 next month in London.'

'Enrique is attractive,' she says.

'Yes, he's like Hugo. They have that same continental olive-coloured skin and brown eyes.'

'Nina King looks as though she's had cosmetic surgery, look at those lips. She's been Botoxed from top to toe. No one is born looking like that. She's like a doll with that waist, and she hardly has any facial expressions,' Tina adds thoughtfully. 'James has short hair now. It suits him.'

I don't reply so she continues, 'In theory, all of these people would be of use for a pyramid scheme. They're either investors, social influencers who blog and people who have a massive following on Insta or Twitter. These are the social media influencers who could potentially turn a business into a huge multi-million-pound investment.'

'I agree, Tina. Think about it. One of the reasons Barack Obama won the presidential election and got into power was because the ordinary person could afford a few dollars for his campaign. Thousands of poor people gave small amounts, sometimes it was all they could afford, maybe ten dollars, and this boosted his campaign fund. Now, if you could get someone as charming or as persuasive as all of these people endorsing the same product, and encourage lots of people to pay small amounts, then it could be massive. It's all about economics – the economy of scale; selling a small volume for a higher price or selling for a lower price to a bigger volume of people.'

'It's frightening.' She lifts her glass and regards me carefully. 'There's a lot at stake, Ronda.'

'I think Hugo is worried. They had no idea this was going on.'

'I think they should just warn them off,' Tina insists. 'If they tell them that James is a scam artist and that he ripped you off and—'

'Hugo says Inspector Joachin wants to wait. They must see what happens next week, and they're going to prepare.'

'How?'

I shrug. 'Hugo wouldn't tell me. He said that unless I was one of their team he couldn't confide in me.'

'So, why not? Become one of their team, Ronda.'

'No.' I turn away, remembering my romantic encounter with Hugo, my cheeks burning.

'You are telling me everything, aren't you?'

'Of course.'

'Are you sure?'

'You know all the important details, Tina.'

'Just one thing,' Tina says. 'What about Daniel? Is he a player in all of this?'

'I don't know. He's certainly charming enough, and maybe by coincidence, he's also another influencer. He's often on TV. People listen to what he says.'

'So what will you do, Ronda?'

'I only want to find James. I want my money back.'

7

# Chapter 7

*'Influence is the new power – if you have influence, you can create a brand.'*
**Michelle Phan**

On Wednesday morning I'm on the road by seven-thirty. The traffic leaving London is horrendous made worse by lashing rain, but as I enter into the county of Kent the clouds part and the low milky sun shines through my filthy windscreen. I set the wipers and sing along to the radio, hoping it will take my mind off the day ahead.

I park in my usual place, beside Daniel's Porsche Cayenne. There's an unmarked white van parked beside it. As I open my car door I'm reminded of last week and how Daniel bounded out of the back door, but today there's no one to greet me, and the kitchen is empty. I walk through the bar area and toward the voices in the dining room. The doors are open.

'Hello? Daniel?' I call.

He appears wearing casual jeans and a jumper.

'Ronda? Is it that time already?'

He glances at his watch and then over his shoulder. He speaks to the man inside. 'You'd better hurry up.' Then he turns his attention to me. 'Pop the coffee on, and I'll be through in a second.'

I do as he asks wondering what's going on and if I could risk taking another look, but then Daniel appears with two men wearing identical black trousers and black sweatshirts. They walk through the kitchen, and Daniel walks with them to the back door.'

I watch them through the window as they climb into the van and drive away.

'Morning,' I say when Daniel strides back inside.

'Sorry about that.'

'Here's your coffee. Everything alright?' I slide a mug across the counter to him.

'All done,' Daniel says, smiling.

'What's all done?'

'I've had the pub debugged. You know, swept to make sure there are no hidden cameras or recording gear.'

'Really, why?'

'It's my policy for private meetings. They pay me good money to feel secure and safe.'

'It's a good idea then,' I reply, thinking it's a bit extreme.

'That's what they pay me for, Ronda. Everything must be top secret.'

'I guess these business deals must be worth a fortune ...'

He looks at me and takes the coffee.

'Thank you. Yes, this one is particularly important, I suppose.'

'The guest list last week was like a who's who.' I grin. 'Pretty impressive. James is incredible. I don't know how he managed to pull all that off. Have you known him long?'

Daniel frowns. 'A year or so.'

'Really.'

That means James knew or met Daniel while we were dating. 'How did you meet?'

'Through Lord Bonner.'

'The disgraced peer?' I joke.

Daniel's frown deepens.   'I don't think he was ever convicted—'

I raise my hand. 'I was joking,' I say, although I wasn't.

Daniel sighs. 'You know what it's like, Ronda. Tell me something. Who gets to the top of the tree without climbing on anyone? Look at any successful businessman or any politician – they've all got dirty hands. They're all open to bribes. They're sent cases of wine so that a supermarket has permission to open. They get a free holiday in the Caribbean so the investor can get building regulations through – they're often coerced and persuaded or financially rewarded to endorse some project or other, and they all make money. You never see a poor politician, do you?'

'No.'

'So, how did you meet James?' He regards me over his coffee mug.

'I'd just finished *Masterchef*, and I was cooking in a restaurant – at a private function in London. James came into the kitchen. He recognised me from the TV programme.' I stop.

I don't tell him how James followed me to three private functions until I'd finally relented and given him my phone number and agreed to have dinner with him.

'He's a charmer, and he's intelligent.' Daniel smiles.

'Do you like his ... investment project?' I probe.

Daniel scratches his nose. 'Well, it's certainly interesting. We'll know more today.' He checks his watch. 'Goodness, is that the time? I'd better get changed.'

\* \* \*

'The menu this week is steak and ale pie, chicken and mushroom pie or salmon stir fry. Dessert is rhubarb crumble or sticky toffee pudding.' Daniel slides a sheet of notepaper toward me. 'I've bought all the fresh produce.'

'Thank you. Who chose the menu?'

Daniel smiles. 'James, of course. He knows how he wants everything.'

I take out my leather knife roll and unfurl it, so it lies open on the counter. The knives are sharp, lethal and immaculate.

James wasn't going to intimidate me this time. Not this week. Last week he'd taken me by surprise. Now I have my own agenda. I'm not sure I want to play the long game that Hugo and Inspector Joachim are interested in. I just want my money.

'Right then, I'd better get busy. I'm just going to set up the screen,' Daniel says.

'Screen?'

'Yes, James is making a presentation before lunch today, so,' Daniel says as an afterthought, 'lunch might be delayed if there are lots of questions.'

'That's fine.'

'Good. Thanks, Ronda. I like working with you. You're very calm under pressure. We'll have to organise something when this is over ...'

I smile. Under pressure? Try cooking in a war zone.

Daniel takes his coffee with him to the dining room, and I'm left thinking about James and the type of presentation he will deliver. If what Hugo tells me is true, then how has James managed to get this project to such an influential level?

I'm busy slicing and chopping, thinking, working on automatic pilot getting some of the prep work done when Billy arrives. He greets me with a wan smile.

'Are you alright, Ronda?'

'Fine.'

He grins. 'You look like you have an agenda with those knives.'

'You're safe, so long as you do a good job.' I smile back.

'Same procedure as last week?' he asks.

'Same procedure, different menu.'

I slide the sheet of paper over towards him and we study it together.

'They've already put in their order?' he says.

'So it seems.'

*James Frampton steak & ale pie*

*Lord Bonner, steak & ale pie*

*Enrique Suarez – salmon stir fry*

*Nina King – salmon stir fry*

*Aiden Moore – steak with mushroom & brandy sauce*

*Gloria – salmon stir fry*

*Prakash Khan – chicken & mushroom pie*

*Prince Abdul – chicken & mushroom pie*

'If you start prepping the meat, I'll get Daisy on the rest of the veg when she arrives.'

'I'm surprised she's late. She's normally so keen.'

Hugo arrives next. This time he's dressed in a grey charcoal suit. There's a navy handkerchief in his top pocket and a pin lapel of a wine bottle on his jacket collar. His eyes are dark, but he smiles brightly. He greets Billy and me like we're old friends.

'Do you know where the key to the cellar is?' Hugo asks.

Billy replies, 'It's normally hanging behind the bar. If not, Daniel will have it.'

'Daniel is in the dining room,' I reply.

'Okay. Great.'

I nod my head at Hugo to wait. I need to tell him about this morning.

Billy is standing at the kitchen sink. His back is turned to us.

I scribble a note to Hugo and slide it across the counter so he can read it.

*What's your mobile number?*

He scribbles it down.

A few minutes later, I take the paper with me to the ladies' bathroom. It's empty. I sit in a cubicle and pull out my iPhone. I add Hugo to my contacts list and flush the paper with his number down the toilet.

I type Hugo a message.

*FYI – Daniel had the place swept for bugs this morning.*

I change into my whites and tie a blue, purple and mauve bandana around my hair. I add eyeliner and mascara and pink lipstick, and I'm washing my hands when my phone pings.

*Thanks, Hx*

He's added a kiss.

When I get back, Daisy is in the kitchen. She looks different and she's already peeling potatoes.

'What are you smiling about, Ronda?' she says. 'You look like you're in love.'

'I don't think so.'

'I love your bandanas. Do you make them?'

'A friend makes them for me. Now, when you've got the potatoes on, can you start the prep for the other veg and the rhubarb? Where's Billy?'

'Having a cigarette.'

'Well, he'll need to come inside now, we have a lot to do.'

The morning flies past with the preparation. Daniel strides in and out, checking the dining table, adding missing items. He's not as organised today, or maybe it's because he had to set up the screen for James, but he seems edgier.

By comparison, Hugo glides in and out, smiling at Daisy, organising wines and while Billy chops and prepares the meat, I fillet the whole fresh salmon.

'Are they really so fussy about what they drink?' Daisy asks.

'Of course.' Hugo grins. He's tipping ice cubes into silver champagne buckets. 'Most of these people have travelled all over the world and have dined in the best restaurants.'

'Did you speak to any of them last week?'

Hugo pretends to think. 'Um, Lord Bonner—'

'The old bloke?'

'He's only fifty,' Billy interrupts laughing. 'He's not a dinosaur.'

'I mean, did you speak to Gloria? Isn't she gorgeous? I tried to get tickets for her concert in London, but it's completely sold out.'

'When is she playing?' Billy asks.

'She's on for three nights at the O2 at the beginning of December. Her concerts have been a massive success in Japan and China, bigger than Lady Gaga. They call her a female Freddie Mercury.' Daisy sighs and her eyes glow.

I realise then that she's straightened her frizzy hair and is proudly showing off a fringe – like Gloria's.

'Is she coming by helicopter today?'

Hugo shrugs. 'Maybe.'

'Can you ask her to have a photograph with me? Can you imagine if I got a selfie?'

'I think the same rules apply as last week,' I say to Daisy. 'I don't think Daniel will be pleased if you approach the guests.'

Daisy turns the corners of her mouth down and continues to chop the vegetables but with more vigour.

'Ronda?'

I look up.

'Have you got a minute?' Daniel is peering around the kitchen door and he nods his head for me to follow him.

I lay down my large santoku and follow him through to the bar. He indicates for me to sit beside him near the window, where there's a clear view of the pub entrance and the lane to the village.

'Could you please do me a favour?' he asks softly.

'I'll try.'

'Daisy was hanging around last week, you know, going to the bathroom hoping to catch a glimpse of the stars ...' He smiles. 'I do understand. I know she likes Gloria, but I can't let her behave like that. This project is important and I don't want anyone to get upset. Can you keep an eye on her for me?'

'I'll try.'

Upset? He must mean James.

He places his hand on my knee.

'When this is all over ...'

I move my knee away. Daniel smiles and continues, 'When this is all over, perhaps we can have dinner together in London?

I know a lovely little restaurant...'

I don't know what to say. I'm shocked.

'I can see I've surprised you, Ronda. I'm sorry, but the thing is, I'd like to get to know you better. Once this is all over, I'll be in a better place to offer you something more substantial, more meaningful.'

I frown. What is Daniel talking about? A business proposition?

He leans forward and whispers, 'If this project comes off, and it's as incredible as James says, then I'll open a restaurant up in town, maybe Soho, and perhaps we can talk about working together?'

I nod cautiously. He frowns and gazes quickly out of the window as if he wants to add something else, so I remain quiet.

His voice lowers, and it's so quiet, I have to lean forward to hear him speak.

'I'm going to be worth a fortune, Ronda, and I'll look after you.'

I'm not sure I've heard him correctly, but then he begins to stroke the inside of my thigh. That's when Hugo walks into the bar, he sees us, and then turns around on his heel and walks out.

* * *

The guests are arriving. I hear them in the hallway, greeting each other. I identify their voices, the deep tones of Lord Bonner, the Indian accent of Prakesh Khan, Prince Abdul, who speaks slowly and Enrique Suarez who is friendly and appears amenable. I imagine him shaking their hands and slapping them on the shoulder.

Last week they weren't even friends. They had no common bond and the atmosphere was subdued by comparison. This week they seem animated. Friendly. There's laughter and camaraderie as if James's joint venture is bonding them as friends or perhaps business colleagues. Last week James had promised to make them millions. More money than they already have, and they seemed to like the idea. Today, he has to convert that promise into hard facts, and I wonder how his business presentation will turn out.

'Nina and Gloria have come in the car together,' Daisy says excitedly, running to the kitchen window while reaching for her iPhone. 'They've driven around the back. She didn't come in her helicopter this week. I might be able to—'

'Daisy, I need you to help me,' I say. 'Can you get me the flour?'

She turns away from the window reluctantly. 'I read this week that Nina has paid over ten thousand dollars on cosmetic surgery.'

'She looks like it.' Billy smiles but doesn't look up.

'I'd pay it, if I had it.' Daisy pouts. 'It's alright for you men. You don't have to bother.'

'That's not true!' Billy protests good-naturedly.

I interrupt their banter. 'You don't need it, Daisy. You're very beautiful, now get the dishes ready for the dessert please.'

'I won't always work in the kitchen, you know. I'll go further than this pub, you know.'

'I know you will.' I watch her laying out the ceramic bowls. 'Now, we need to get some whisky from Hugo for the dessert.'

'He was in the cellar a few minutes ago,' Billy says.

'He's in the bar now, so I'll go.' Daisy's smile brightens and in a few seconds, she's left the kitchen before I can say a word to stop her.

It amazes me how Billy and Daisy both seem to be aware of where everyone is at any one time. They both randomly disappear, but by the same token, they also seem to have a sixth sense of what's going on everywhere.

Billy shakes his head. 'Daisy's enamoured with wealth and glamour, but I suppose it's normal at her age.'

'She's young,' I agree. 'And easily impressed.'

'Gloria's an amazing singer, and her concerts have been incredible, so at least she admires someone worthy of it all.' Billy works as he talks.' Daisy has a good work ethic, but she's easily distracted this week which I guess is understandable.'

I add seasoning to the pies, and suddenly I'm aware of someone entering the kitchen.

'Don't forget to add the ale to my steak pie.' James's tone is friendly and playful.

I look up, and James is staring at me.

'You did the last time, Ronda, and it was awful.'

After threatening me last week, he's now pretending to be my friend. I refuse to join in his banter.

'I didn't.' I coolly turn my back.

He may have hired the pub, but Daniel employed me, and I don't have to be polite to him.

James moves toward me and leans on the counter beside me. 'You've probably been wondering why I want you to cook for us?'

'No. I haven't given it any thought.'

I don't look at him, but I sense Billy smiling.

James moves closer. He's wearing his familiar aftershave, and I'm aware of him near me, and I suddenly remember how he made me feel. He was exciting, thrilling, and there was always a sense of danger with him. Sexually, he was liberated and confident. I remember his touch. He knew how to arouse me, pleasure me, and make me feel as though I was the only women he'd ever want. He'd made me feel special, loved and desired. He'd been my hero. The dashing, handsome gentleman, who'd opened doors for me or pulled out a chair. He was a man who walked by my side nearest the road on the pavement. His chivalry had eventually won me over. Now he is at my elbow. Before, he would have pulled me gently into his arms, kissed me passionately and caressed me, luring me into the bedroom. Now, I move away. My hands are smelling of the gutted salmon, and I wash them at the sink.

He follows me.

Billy moves to the fridge at the far end of the room. He's out of earshot.

'You owe me money.' I lower my voice. 'You stole from me. You're a thief.'

James smiles. 'You'll get it back.'

'When?'

'When this is over, a couple of weeks.'

'I'd better.'

'Or what?'

'I'll go to the police.'

'Oh, Ronda.' He grins. 'You do make me laugh. We were together. You gave it to me, remember?'

'You stole it.'

'You're just sore because I didn't turn up on our wedding day, but I couldn't help it.'

I gaze at him, shocked he's even mentioning it.

'The thing is,' he continues, 'I had an accident, and then all this happened, and I've been swamped. But you can see, I've never forgotten you.' He strokes my arm.

I pull away.

'What's wrong? You used to love me touching you, Ronda,' he whispers.

'Not anymore.'

'You will when this is over.'

'You're a liar. You didn't have an accident. You stole my money. You used me and then you left. I don't know why you want me back in your life or why you recommended me for this work, but I'm sure it's not for my benefit because everything is always about you and what you want.'

James grins. 'How right you are.'

'So, let me guess.' I think quickly. 'I'm assuming that as Daniel has employed me to work here, it's a cover for you. You'd tell the police I knew all about your project, and that I gave you my money and there are no hard feelings between us, that's why I agreed to cater for everyone.'

James folds his arms casually and stares at me with a smile on his lips.

'It's another way of using me for your own gains,' I add.

Billy comes back to the counter. He doesn't look at us, but he must be aware of our exchange.

'Clever girl, Ronda. You are your father's daughter.'

I want to punch him. I'd told him about my strict upbringing and my father's military background because I'd trusted him.

I turn away to dry my hands, but James leans over my shoulder, and his breath tickles my ear when he whispers, 'Do as I say, Ronda. And you'll get your money.'

'Why don't I believe you?' I hiss back. 'You lying, thieving toad.'

He squeezes my bottom. I turn around to thump him, but

he's gone, and it's Billy who is staring back at me with a look of mild amusement on his face.

# 8

# Chapter 8

*'The humblest individual exerts some influence, either for good or evil, upon others.'*
**Henry Ward Beecher**

I'm simultaneously checking the rhubarb dessert at the same time as making sure that the steak and ales pies are perfectly cooked. Then I marinate the salmon in a hoisin sauce.

'The pies need a light and crispy top. We mustn't burn them,' I say to Daisy, who leans over my shoulder and gazes into the oven.

'If I could cook like you, then I could cater for all these sorts of people,' she says.

I smile. It sounds so simple when she says it, and I'm not about to disillusion her.

'I could cook for Gloria,' she says, dreamily.

'Wouldn't you prefer to cook for Harry Styles or Ed Sheeran?' Billy teases, and Daisy pokes out her tongue at him.

'I don't fancy Gloria,' she explains to me. 'I just want her to be my best friend.'

'Flights of fancy,' Billy laughs.

'Did you get the alcohol for me, Daisy?'

'Oh, not yet. I'll go now.'

'No, you finish slicing the vegetables, I want them all the same size for the stir fry, and then help Billy. I'll only be a few minutes.'

I'm determined to find something out today. I want to know what's going on. What is James really up to?

I walk down the hallway – the bar area is empty. I check the bathroom and it's also empty, so I make my way to where the guests are all gathered in the dining room. The double doors are shut, so I place my ear to the wood and I can hear the murmur of James's voice. I imagine him standing in front of the screen, confident and authoritative. I can't hear the details, and I guess that Hugo is inside listening.

There's a noise. I turn.

Standing behind me is the bodyguard from last week. He's the driver for Prakash. He's tall, broad, Middle Eastern-looking and he's not smiling.

'I need a bottle of whisky for the dessert,' I whisper. 'I wanted to ask Hugo the sommelier.'

He stands staring at me, his face impassive, his broad shoulders blocking out the light from the bar.

'Well, it appears they're busy in there. I can't get hold of Hugo. I'll have to help myself.'

I walk toward him to brazen it out, and reluctantly he moves aside. He follows me into the bar where, behind the counter, I check the rows of bottles, calming myself, making my breathing regular while surreptitiously watching him in the mirror as I check the labels.

I find a bottle of whisky. I lift it with exaggerated pleasure.

Then I ignore the bodyguard who has made it his task to watch and follow me, and I head back to the kitchen.

'Alright, Ronda?' Billy asks.

'The bodyguard is hanging around near the bar, and he surprised me.'

'He was there earlier,' Daisy says. 'But I ignored him. I just smiled and went to the bathroom. It's not against the law, is it? We need to have a wee.'

I check the flavour of the gravy, dipping in my finger and licking it. 'More salt.'

'Yes, chef.' Billy smiles.

I check the time.

James's presentation is running over time, and it's almost one-fifteen.

I grate ginger for the rhubarb syllabub compote. It will give it an extra spicy kick, and I fork it through the creamy filling, pleased the meringue top will fit perfectly on the dish like a jaunty tilted hat.

'Daisy, bring me the meringues.'

Suddenly the dining-room doors open, there's a flurry of activity in the hallway, and voices break out.

A few minutes later, Daniel appears.

'Right, the presentation is over. They're having a break for ten minutes. The ladies have gone to the bathroom. Now, are we all ready?'

'Yes.'

He smiles, and there's something in his expression that I'm still thinking about as I plate the dishes. It's a confident, excited look. It's the smug smile of satisfaction from a man mulling over his fortune. It's the look of a man who realises he's won the lottery but he hasn't yet claimed his prize. He hovers around us, not helping, not seeing anything, but lost in his own fantasy inside his head.

James's presentation must have gone well, and I wonder if all the guests are equally as impressed. I have a sudden urge to know more. Is James about to be the new crypto king and head of a multinational investment company?

'Ready?' I ask.

Billy nods.

'Let's plate up.'

Billy works alongside me, and carefully I add the decoration to each plate, balancing the pastry tops, laying the bundled vegetables uniformly beside the potato wedges. Daisy pours the mushroom and brandy sauce into a tiny jug for the steak, and I check Billy's actions as he turns the frying steak.

I toss the salmon and vegetable stir fry for the last time and place the crispy salmon skin on the side.

'Right, service,' I call.

Hugo appears on cue.

Daniel checks the dishes against the seating plan.

'Let's go,' I say.

The atmosphere in the dining room is vastly different to last week when there was an air of nervous excitement and anticipation. This week, in stark contrast, the conversation is flowing animatedly. The guests forget we're serving a meal and their discussions and exclamations continue as we place the plates on the table, we're scarcely noticed. I return to the kitchen with the words I've overheard lingering in my head. They're buzz words like; global currency, investment, quadrupled, opportunity, prime, and safe, unlike Bitcoin. James's voice echoes in my head; influencers, spreading the news, encouragement, the future.

While the guests are eating their main course, I go to the bathroom. I need a break from the kitchen to think.

In the cubicle I text Tina.

*The presentation is over. It seems a success and James is beaming like the cat who got the cream.*

I text Hugo.

*I hope you'll update me.*

He doesn't reply and I don't expect an answer. He's busy in the dining room serving fine wines.

As I come out of the bathroom, I'm distracted by whispering voices in the bar. Curious, I tiptoe closer, my heart banging in my chest, and I peer around the little nook.

Prince Abdul is leaning casually on the bar. He's taken a cheroot from his pocket, and he lights it slowly. He appears to be on his own, but then a head appears from behind the bar. Hugo must have gone down to the cellar. He appears with a bottle of red wine wrapped in meshed gold, and he raises it triumphantly.

'I knew there was one down there.' Hugo smiles.

Prince Abdul reaches for the bottle, but instead of taking it he places his hand on Hugo's arm and pulls him slowly closer.

I hold my breath.

They lean forward. Their heads are almost touching. Prince Abdul whispers something to Hugo, and there's something in his manner, the way his mouth moves and the gentle caress of his fingers on Hugo's arm that makes my heart bang. Prince Abdul with his sleepy eyes leans closer and places a kiss near Hugo's mouth.

I turn away. I exhale, and my mouth is dry like sandpaper. My throat is raw and my eyes are burning. I want to shout, but instead, I turn and creep slowly away like the interloper that I am, ashamed to have witnessed an intimate moment between the two men.

* * *

I'm finishing the puddings, concentrating, directing Billy and Daisy, and we're almost ready to plate up when Daisy gasps. Thinking she's done something wrong, I turn around.

Nina is standing in the doorway.

'Hi,' she drawls. 'I just wanted to see where all the action takes place.'

She moves into the kitchen with familiarity and I can see Daisy is impressed.

Nina says, 'That stir fry was amazing. What did you do to the salmon?'

Daisy smoothes down her fringe and smiles. 'Well—'

'Daisy, get me a small spoon.'

'Yes, chef.'

Billy tries to ignore Nina, but it's very hard to look away as she drapes herself across the kitchen counter. Her red hair is falling seductively across her enchanting breasts. She knows she's having an effect on Daisy and she seems to be enjoying it. Even Billy is falling under her spell.

'You might want to be careful; the counter is dirty.' I nod at the spilt sauce.

She rubs at the dirty spot on the sleeve of her cream blouse. 'It'll come out.' She seems unfazed.

I ignore her and continue issuing orders to Billy and Daisy, through hand signals, looks and commands.

'You're just in time,' Nina calls. 'Come and see how they do it, Gloria.'

Beside me, Daisy gasps. She's reaching into her pocket, and I guess she's about to produce her phone.

'Daisy, I need a larger spoon.'

Daisy blinks as Gloria, world-renowned superstar and singer, glides into the kitchen. She smiles at Nina.

'James is looking for you,' Gloria says.

'I won't be a moment. I wanted to take a look at this, as I'm thinking of blogging about celebrity catering. Come and see.'

Daisy is rooted to the floor. She stares at Gloria like she's a goddess.

Billy plates up the small cubes of cheese while I prepare the garnish.

'Can I interview you?' Nina asks me.

'Yes, but not right now.'

Nina laughs. 'If I give you my card?'

'That's fine.'

Billy blinks at me as if he thinks I should do or say something, but I'm cool. I don't care about her interview. Not right now. I want them all out of my kitchen.

'I love your music,' Daisy says breathlessly to Gloria.

Gloria rewards her with a perfect smile and white teeth. Today she's wearing a richly coloured purple, green and black blouse with black suede trousers and silver boots. She's glamorous and effortlessly beautiful, as she smiles at Daisy.

Then Hugo's voice is behind me. He's standing at the door.

'Ladies, James is looking for you.'

'That's what I told Nina.' Gloria's Canadian voice is smoky and seductive, and I realise that's why she is so popular, she does have an incredible voice.

'That looks amazing,' Gloria says to me.

'It will be when it's finished,' Billy replies, and then he

blushes, realising he's spoken aloud.

'Please, sit down in the dining room, and then Ronda can finish off.' Hugo will understand they are in my way, and he does his best to usher the ladies from the kitchen.

After they've gone, Daisy giggles excitedly. 'Did you see that? Gloria stood here. Only an inch away from me.'

'She's smaller than I thought she'd be,' Billy says, grinning.

'She's gorgeous, don't you think? Do you think I can ask her for tickets to her concert?'

'No!' Billy and I say in unison.

Billy turns to me. 'Will you call Nina? She's very keen on watching you cook. It could be an amazing opportunity.'

'If she gives me her card, I might. Right,' I call. 'Service.'

* * *

Billy is preparing coffee and various flavoured teas while Daisy begins the process of cleaning the dishes, so I take a few minutes to myself and step outside in the fresh air to think and to clear my head.

What is James playing at? To seduce people into believing his scheme for making people rich, that Hugo calls a cheap pyramid scheme?

I pull out my phone and google Bitcoin.

I scan the text. Some investment journalists view it as an investment and others as a wild speculative bet. The problem is that digital currency is not backed by any tangible assets, so as a result, it's difficult to value, and this makes the share price volatile. It's not ruled or governed by a central body, so its operation can change, which means that some investors can lose out. Investment in this digital currency is known, in serious investment circles, as *a get rich quick scheme to make money.*

It's the antithesis of a serious investment which is usually to invest or plough money into a dynamic business and reap the reward in the long term. So why are this group falling for James's plan?

* * *

I'm standing at the back door near the kitchen and I'm amused that Peanut, my humble Fiat 500, is parked amongst Aiden Moore's Bugatti, Prince Abdul's Lamborghini and Enrique Suarez's Goldwing.

I take a deep breath and venture further round to the back of the pub. I look over the gardens and fields to where Gloria's helicopter landed a week ago. Now sheep are grazing peacefully.

Parked behind the building, Lord Bonner's chauffeur has reclined his car seat and appears to be dozing, but Prakash's bodyguard who was inside the pub is now leaning casually on the fence.

It amazes me, the amount of money they all have.

How did James get involved with these people?

And, worse still, how could they possibly trust him?

A part of me feels sick. I trusted him. He fooled me. I know what James is like. I know he's a conman and a thief.

But what about Hugo, and Prince Abdul – how well do they know each other?

'Ronda?'

I turn at the sound of my name.

'James, what do you want?' I copy his whispered tone.

He giggles and takes my arm, pulling me closer to the wall. His breath smells of expensive wine.

'I thought I saw you lingering out here. You'll never believe it; they love my plan.' He pulls me into the recess of the wall. 'They think it's brilliant. They love me. They think I'm a genius.'

'You haven't told me what this is all about.'

He frowns. 'Haven't I? You know what it is, it's the Internet currency. I told you about it.'

'You said you were writing software.'

'I was, but that was before.'

'Before what?'

'Before I met some significant and like-minded people. People who believe in what I'm doing.' He laughs. 'This will change the world. It will change how we do business – forever.'

I shake my head. I can't believe him.

'Ronda, this is an incredible investment and guess what, I thought it all up. It's my idea.'

He's lying. I know he is. I want to shout that it's pyramid selling and that he's ripping people off and it's nothing to be proud of, but I don't.

'How did you meet all these people?' I hiss, wanting to learn more.

'It's easy.' He grins. 'You meet one, they like you, they talk about you, and then they all come flocking to you. They all want money. They're greedy.' James is giggling now.

I shake my head. 'It's not all about money. It can't be.'

He nods enthusiastically. 'But it is. It's simple. They all like the good things in life and to get those things you need money. They all *like* money, and they want to be the first to tell the world about how to make it. They are influencers, and they like to be the first ones to let people in on a secret that will make them rich. They want to lead. They want to know what's going on, and give advice and—'

'But it's illegal.'

James pulls away with a shocked look on his face. 'What's illegal?'

'What you're doing.'

'You don't know that, why are you saying that, Ronda?'

'Because I know you, James. You're scamming them.'

He grabs my upper arm and squeezes me tightly.

'Don't you dare say that to me, or repeat it to anyone else. Not when I've got eight cheques in my pocket, each for three hundred thousand dollars.'

'What?' I gasp.

James lets me go.

'How much?'

'Three hundred thousand dollars, they've all paid me. They're not stupid people, Ronda. This is a massive investment, and it's me.' He pokes his thumb at his chest. 'It's me that's giving them this opportunity. It's an investment of a lifetime. I can quadruple their money in three months.'

I stare at James.

'Close your mouth, Ronda. I'm not as thick as you think I am.'

'I never thought you were stupid. Quite the opposite, James. You're *very* clever.'

He seems to think that remark is a compliment. He straightens his shoulders, and the swaggering smile comes back to his lips.

'I'll give you your poxy bit of money unless you want me to invest it for you. You can have a share in this.'

'No, I'll have it back. I want my money.'

'I can give you four times its value in six months.'

'I'll take my fifty grand today, now, thank you.' I hold out my hand.

'I can give you two hundred thousand—'

'No. I don't want it. I want my money today.'

He bats my hand away. 'You're so stubborn, Ronda. That's always been a problem with you.'

Prakash's bodyguard walks past. He stares at us.

I stare defiantly at him.

I say to James, 'Well, let's not go into your problems, shall we?'

'Baby, you have really missed out on this. You'll be kicking yourself in three months.' He grins at me and turns to walk away.

'What about my money?' I call.

'You'll have to wait,' he replies over his shoulder. 'I'm a busy man.'

Prakash's expressionless bodyguard leans against his car and watches me as I follow James back inside the pub.

# 9

# Chapter 9

*'It would be difficult to exaggerate the degree to which we are influenced by those we influence.'*
**Eric Hoffer**

When I'm back inside the kitchen, Daisy whispers, 'Daniel caught me going into the bathroom, and he sent me back to the kitchen. He's furious.'

'You know the rules,' I reply.

'I know, but I can't help it if I need to pee—'

'Then you need to see a doctor, Daisy. You've wanted to go four times in the past three hours, and that's not normal.' I smile. 'Besides, Daniel isn't stupid. He knows you're desperate to get a selfie with Gloria.'

'Is it that obvious?'

I grin. 'Yes. But is it worth making him angry and losing your job?'

Billy comes into the kitchen from the bar looking flustered.

Daisy asks, 'What's happened? Has he been awful to you too?'

'Well, I was here in the kitchen and Hugo said he wanted my help to carry a few crates of wine to Prince Abdul's car but then ...' His voice trails off, and he shakes his head.

'What?' Daisy encourages him to continue.

'It's weird. That bodyguard who is always hanging around followed me down to the cellar. He watched me pass up the crates to Hugo, and we carried them to Prince Abdul's Lamborghini.'

'Well, what's wrong with that?'

'Well, Daniel didn't seem very happy. It was as if he had to do it. He looks very fed up.'

'Really?' Daisy says. 'That's probably why he was so grumpy with me.'

'What about Hugo?' I ask.

Billy frowns. 'He was just doing his job, I suppose.'

'It's all a bit strange,' Daisy adds. 'I overheard Nina asking Gloria if she was giving James a cheque.'

'A cheque for what?' Billy asks.

'I think they're investing in James's project.' Daisy smiles at me, and when I raise my eyebrows, she shrugs.

Billy looks up. 'Did she give him a cheque?'

'I think they all did.'

'Daisy,' I ask, 'How do you know all this?'

'Well, I put bits together and I overheard some stuff when I went for a pee.'

'Like what? Give me an example.' I want to find out as much as I can from them both.

'Well Aiden, the gorgeous guy who looks like Idris Elba, isn't pleased, but he wrote a cheque, and I think he might have done it because everyone else did, and James told him that he could have it back anytime he likes if he isn't sure. There's a cooling-off period of a week—'

Daniel comes into the kitchen, looking flustered and edgy. He sees that we're cleaning up, but it seems as if he's using the kitchen as a place to hide.

'Is everything alright?' I ask.

'They'll be going soon, so we won't clear the dining room until they've gone. Daisy, you can go home, and you too, Billy. Ronda, will you stay and help me clear up in there?'

'Yes.'

'I don't mind staying,' Daisy protests, but Daniel shakes his head. 'Go home now, please. I'll see you tomorrow.'

'Are we open as normal tomorrow?' Daisy pulls off her apron and flings it on the kitchen counter. She's clearly not happy to go home when her singing idol is still here.

'Of course.' Daniel watches while she pulls on her coat.

Her eyes are dark, and she's doesn't button it up. 'Bye, Ronda. You know how much I've loved working with you?'

'I do, Daisy. Thanks for all your help today. I really appreciate it.'

'Well, I'm glad someone does.' She grabs her bag and slams out of the kitchen door without a backwards glance.

Billy pulls off his apron more slowly, and reluctantly he takes his coat from the hook.

'Thanks, Ronda.'

'Thank you, Billy. You did a great job.'

With one final look, he gives Daniel a cheeky two-fingered salute from his temple. 'See you tomorrow, boss. Bye, Ronda.'

'Bye, Billy.'

The door closes, and Daniel strides around the kitchen and looks out of the window.

'Are you alright?' I ask.

Daniel shakes his head. 'I'm fine.'

I pick up Daisy's apron and look at the remainder of the dishes near the sink to clean plus the dessert dishes and glasses in the dining room, and I try not to sigh.

'That was all a bit dramatic,' I say. 'Was it necessary?'

'I'm not sure, but I think it was for the best.'

'Why?'

Daniel turns from the window. 'Ronda, have you noticed anything suspicious?'

My instinct is to laugh. The whole set-up is suspicious.

'Suspicious? No, not really. Like what?'

'Right, thank you.' Daniel storms out leaving me alone, clearly frustrated that I haven't given him the answer he was looking for but I'm not playing his game. He's on James's side.

I place the pots on the side and turn off the dishwasher. The first load is finished, so I begin to unstack it.

Suspicious; I laugh aloud. I'd like to have said to Daniel; *well, apart from my thieving ex, turning up out of the blue with a scheme that he couldn't possibly have designed and who is ripping off a bunch of influential celebrities, an undercover policeman from Europol, and a bodyguard who looks as intimidating as a criminal in a fourth-rate movie – there's nothing at all suspicious going on around here.*

\* \* \*

I miss Daisy, not just because I have to wash up, that doesn't bother me, but I like the way she and Billy knew what was going on. Now I'm alone and working methodically through the jobs; cleaning up and trying to assess the situation out in the bar and the dining room. There are conversations taking place between the investors, in smaller groups, privately, and with James.

According to James, they've all given him a cheque. They've all invested in his project. Is he lying to me? But then Daisy seems to think that was true too.

From my vantage point at the sink at the kitchen window, I see the cars begin to leave. First, Lord Bonner and his chauffeur then Enrique on his Goldwing and after them, Aiden Moore in his black Bugatti.

I'm cleaning pots and pans, and I'm putting them away when Hugo appears carrying dirty dishes and glasses.

'Thank you.'

'Did Daniel send Daisy and Billy home?'

'Yes.'

'Good.'

I look up sharply. 'Why?'

'They were too nosy.'

He leaves the dirty dishes on the kitchen counter.

Hugo looks at me, and I see it then. Why hadn't realised it before? A good-looking man, smart, clean, handsome, long eyelashes, beautiful lips. Of course, he wouldn't be interested in me. He had kissed me in Scotland because it was a cover-up, but since then he'd not attempted to flirt with me. Of course, he hadn't. Once again, it was my fault; my lousy choice of men.

'Is everything alright?' I ask him.

He smiles reassuringly. 'There's only Nina, Gloria and Prince Abdul in the dining room. Once they've gone, I'll clear the rest.'

'Fine.'

'What didn't you want Daisy and Billy to see?' I ask, but he ignores me.

'I'll come back when I can.'

I'm alone, restacking the dishwasher, when my phone pings.

110

I pull it from my pocket, and to my delight, Daisy is sending me the images she took earlier this morning.

*This is a secret*, DX. She types.

I smile—what a star.

\* \* \*

I don't hear Nina. She comes quietly into the kitchen while I'm bending down, organising the pans for the regular chef in the morning. When I look up, she's smiling. Her skin is rigid across her enhanced cheeks, but she bares her teeth and her eyes gleam. She pulls her hair behind her ears, and she reminds me of a slinky golden fox.

'I want to leave you my card, Ronda.'

'Thank you.'

'Better still, if you give me your number or your Insta account, we can be friends?'

'I don't have an Insta account.'

She looks horrified. 'My goodness, you're missing out, massively.'

'Probably.' I stand up.

'I could film you, you know, cooking dishes. An online blog. What do you think?'

'I'll give it some thought.'

'You have a face for TV, you're pretty, and those green eyes are quite remarkable.'

'Thank you.'

'Are they natural, or are you wearing coloured lenses?'

'They're mine.'

'You have a calm presence. There's a gravitas about you, yet there's a hint of fun, and your humour comes across. That's why you were also very popular on *Masterchef.* You were my favourite almost from the beginning.'

'I can't imagine why.'

'It was the mini-documentary they did about you. I remember it well. The one where you talked about your army career, and you spoke about how they posted you to the war zones. Didn't you save that chap's life in Afghanistan?'

I turn away, not wanting to be reminded of losing my other friends – the three men I couldn't save. It had been a direct hit on the canteen. We had been lucky. I had been lucky.

'I was hoping people would remember me for my culinary skills.'

Nina ignores my sarcasm and asks, 'How well do you know James?'

'Not very,' I lie.

'Do you know anything about this project?'

I shake my head. 'I wasn't at the presentation.'

'No.' She regards me thoughtfully. 'You'd be a good influencer, though. It would be best if you thought about it. Are you on social media at all?'

'No.'

'You should be, Ronda. It will improve your status. I have over 50 million followers.'

'That's incredible.'

'Well, that's what I thought, but Gloria has more, even more followers than Lady Gaga, who has over 81 million.'

'Really?'

She ticks them off on her fingers. 'Cristiano Ronaldo, Taylor Swift, Justin Bieber, they're all on it. This is how you keep your fans up to date with what's going on. It's incredible. You should think about it.'

'I will.'

'Right, I'd better see if Gloria is ready to go. I think Prince Abdul is quite besotted by her. She's off to Paris in the morning for her concert in the evening, and she's asked me to go with her. If you had an Insta or Twitter account you'd see all the pictures I post.' She pauses at the door. 'Think about it, Ronda. You'd make a lot of money, you could write cookbooks, and all sorts, there are so many opportunities. I could help you if you like.'

'Thank you.'

Gloria appears at the door. 'Are you ready to go, Nina?'

'Yes,' she replies to her and then she turns and waves at me. 'Bye, Ronda.'

'Bye, Nina.'

In the hallway, I hear Gloria ask, 'Have you given James your cheque?'

'Yes.'

'Good. Me too.'

* * *

'It's just James, and Prakesh in the bar now.' Daniel brings in glasses from the dining room. 'The others have all gone. It's been busy. There were quite a lot of details to finalise. You can clear up in there now.'

'Okay.'

'I'm sorry, Ronda. But thank you for cleaning up.'

I go in and out of the dining room, clearing, organising and arranging as if it was my own house. I imagine the place as it usually is, a small and intimate restaurant, and tomorrow it will be back to normal. Today, the screen is still on the far wall, and I imagine that James used a Wi-Fi connection to link his presentation. I look in the corner at the bar and wonder where Hugo would have stood to watch. He'd know all the details now, and he would have seen everyone handing over cheques to James.

Why hadn't they asked Hugo to leave the room?

I pick up an ashtray with a partly lit cheroot. I imagine Prince Abdul's sleepy eyes; then I shake my head; it's best not to dwell on the images in my head.

I go back to the kitchen with a full tray. I stack the dishwasher and turn at a sound by the door.

James is watching me.

'Have you got my money?' I ask, wiping my hands on a tea towel.

He walks over to the kitchen counter and pulls open his jacket and pulls out a brown envelope from his inside pocket.

'You didn't believe me, did you?'

He places the envelope on the counter.

'What's that? My money?' I walk toward the counter.

He pulls out eight cheques and lays them on the counter. All are signed and dated with the same amount, three hundred thousand dollars, made out to INTmon Ltd. I check the signatures on the cheques and they match the names of the guests. There's even one from Daniel.

'That doesn't look like my thirty thousand pounds cash.'

'It's far more than that, Ronda. This is me on the road to being the first trillionaire.'

'They don't exist.'

He nods. 'They do, and it will be me, and do you know why? Because these people believe in me. They trust me. I'm going to make them millions, and they know it. Instant success.'

'The cheques might bounce.' I grin. I want to upset him.

'Do you know what this is? Eight by three hundred thousand? It's 2.4 million dollars, Ronda. So, I'll give you your money. I'm not a thief. I'm an investor.'

'What happens when it all falls apart?'

'It won't.'

'What happens when they realise you're a conman and you can't deliver what you've promised – when it all goes wrong.'

He looks puzzled. 'It can't.'

'It might.'

'There's nothing you can do, Ronda. You missed playing your ace card. You could have gone to the police months ago, but you haven't got what it takes anymore. You couldn't even do that.'

'I wanted to protect your mother.'

He laughs. 'You bottled it. That's the real reason you left the army, wasn't it?'

I stare at him.

He collects the cheques together like they're a deck of cards, and puts them back in the envelope and then back inside his inner pocket.

'You see, Ronda. I know all about you. I know your darkest secrets. I used to hear you screaming in your sleep. I heard you talking, night after night, in your dreams. You should get it sorted, do you know that? It's called PTSD.'

I grip the tea towel I'm holding.

'You might have saved one officer, Ronda, but the other three died, didn't they? And you blame yourself. Poor Ronda. Injured, with shrapnel in her back and she pretended she couldn't do any more.'

He turns away from me and I reach for my leather roll of

Japanese knives.

He pauses at the door. 'They died because of you, Ronda. It was all *your* fault.'

I react instinctively. I take the blade of my large santoku between my thumb and index finger, and as I've practised so many times, I throw it at him. James ducks quickly out, and the blade slices into the closed door.

* * *

'Would you like a drink, Ronda?' Daniel asks.

He moves behind the bar with easy familiarity and he appears calmer now than earlier this afternoon.

'I'm fine, thanks.'

'You must be exhausted. You're welcome to stay the night, upstairs.' He smiles.

'Thank you, but I'd better get back to Molly.'

'How old is your daughter?'

'Molly is my dog.'

'Ah.' Daniel grins. 'I just assumed because I have children everyone does.'

I don't reply. I don't ask him how many he has or how old they are or where they are now.

'Well, I need a brandy. Will you sit with me for a while before you go?' He nods at the table beside the fire. He's thrown on an extra log.

'Has everyone gone?'

Daniel nods.

'I didn't say goodbye to Hugo.'

'He got a lift with Prince Abdul.'

'What about his car?'

'He'll come back for it tomorrow.'

'Why?'

Daniel frowns. 'Prince Abdul was a little hesitant about everything and James wanted to keep him sweet, so he insisted I gave Prince Abdul a few crates of the finest claret I use for special guests.'

'A few crates? I hope James is paying you for it?'

'He says he will, but to be honest, this deal he's put together will be so lucrative I won't worry.'

'Really?'

I sit down. I stare at Daniel, then at the bar, where Prince Abdul had kissed Hugo earlier this afternoon. My mind is reeling. Has he gone home with him?

Daniel slides into the seat beside me. 'Are you upset?'

'No.'

'You look sad.'

'I'm tired.'

'It's been an emotional day,' Daniel agrees.

'Has it?' I ask.

'Well, sort of, I hadn't expected to join in as I did with the guests, but James insisted, and as it turns out, I'm fortunate to have been included ...'

'Good.'

'Do you know about James's project?'

'No.'

Daniel sips his brandy slowly and stretches out his legs like a contented man. 'Well, you'll know all about it next week.'

'Next week?'

'Yes, sorry, I did mean to ask you. It's the last meeting. Next Wednesday. It's going to be quite a special event.'

'Why?'

Daniel smiles. 'I'm sworn to secrecy.'

'Why next week?'

'James wanted to make sure the cheques have been cashed before he reveals the big surprise.'

'What's the surprise?'

Daniel grins. 'He wouldn't say, but I have a feeling that some exceptional people will be here.'

# 10

# Chapter 10

*'Blessed is the influence of one true, loving human soul on another.'*
**George Eliot**

'Here you go.'

Tina kisses my cold cheek and hands me a brown paper parcel which I take distractedly. I'm busy looking for Molly, who's disappeared into the bushes.

'She's probably after a rabbit,' I say.

The packet is too big to fit in my pocket, so I walk with it clutched under my arm. My hands are dug deep into my coat pockets and I've pulled the collar across my throat. It's colder in the park today.

'So, you're going to meet the future outlaws?' I joke.

Tina smiles. 'Graham's desperate for me to meet them and I can't keep saying no.'

'He's keen then?'

Tina shrugs. 'He seems to be.'

'How do you feel?'

'Graham is lovely. He's more than I thought he'd ever be; he's kind, loving and generous.'

'And?'

Tina grins. 'I'm scared that he might be the one.'

I link my arm through hers. 'How exciting. I'm thrilled for you.'

'I hope they like me.'

'They will love you.'

'We'll see. So, what about you, Ronda? You've recovered from last Wednesday then?'

'Just about. I could have killed James.'

'What's new?' she grins.

'I mean really killed him. I threw a knife at him.'

'I take it you missed?' She grins.

'He ducked out of the kitchen door. Lucky for him.'

'Lucky for you! Don't go to prison, Ronda. I might need you as a bridesmaid.'

'I'm going to get my money and I don't care how I do it.'

Tina frowns. 'Did you read about Daniel in the Sunday papers?'

'No. What did the newspapers say about him?'

'He's lost his TV contract.'

'Why?'

'He said he has a new business venture and that he decided to leave, but rumour has it that he's been aggressive recently with the crew behind the scenes and he regularly has tantrums.'

'That's why his wife left him.'

'How do you know?'

'Daisy told me.'

'Ah, the lovely Daisy. Did she send you any more photos?'

I pull out my iPhone and pass it to her. Tina slows her pace to look at the pictures. She's wearing a red beret and black coat, whereas I'm in my old dog walking jacket and trainers. She looks successful and sophisticated, and I look as though I've spent the night sleeping rough in the park.

It's stopped raining, and the sun is bursting out from behind a cloud. It's midmorning and the park is busy with a few joggers and an optimistic family with young toddlers, on a bench, eating an early picnic.

Tina flicks through the images slowly, and then she stops.

'This one?'

'That's Prince Abdul and Hugo driving off together in his Lamborghini. She must have waited, hiding along the road.'

'She's like a detective.'

'No, she's just a kid. Daniel sent her and Billy home early because they were both in the way. Every time he went to the bar she was there, hoping to meet Gloria, and then Billy helped Hugo carry a few crates of wine to Prince Abdul's car. Daniel was as angry as a bull.'

'Why?'

'Presumably, the prince was wavering about investing in the project and James wanted to keep him happy. He insisted Daniel give him the wine to take away.'

'Like a bribe?'

'More of a sweetener.'

'But he wrote a cheque in the end?'

'They all wrote one. James took great delight in laying them all out for me to see.'

Tina widens an image with her thumb and forefinger. 'Ooh, Prince Charming.'

'Prince Abdul? He's not even attractive.'

'I meant Hugo. He's very handsome.' Tina lifts the screen

closer to her eyes for a better look.

'He's not interested in me.'

Tina looks at me. 'Are you sure?'

'Yes.'

'Is that why you've been so grumpy recently and didn't want to come for lunch yesterday?'

'No.'

'Graham cooked coq au vin. He was desperate to impress you. It was his own recipe.'

I sigh. 'It's you Graham should be impressing.'

'Oh, he's done that already.' Tina giggles.

I snatch my phone from her hand. 'I don't want to know.'

I scroll through the images and Tina grins.

'Umm.' I turn off my phone.

'And you think Hugo's not interested in you.'

'I know he isn't.'

I glance up at Tina, but she's distracted.

'I think you're very wrong,' she says slowly.

'Well, I'm not.' I'm adamant, and Tina wasn't going to get me interested in any men again. 'Besides, I'm not going to date anyone for at least five years.'

I pocket my phone and walk over to the row of bushes and shrubs. 'Molly?' I call. 'Molly? Where is she, Tina?'

'I think she's found a friend.' Tina smiles.

I follow Tina's gaze.

Molly is sitting at the feet of a man in a dark trench coat. He's smiling at me.

'Well, *hello*, Hugo,' Tina whispers seductively beside me. 'Goodness me, he's gorgeous, Ronda.'

* * *

After a quick introduction, Tina makes her excuses. She's not a criminal lawyer for nothing, and she knows when she's not wanted. Although she met Inspector Joachin in a pub last August, she can tell by Hugo's face that he wants to speak to me privately. He looks worried and eager to talk to me in private.

'I'm sorry, Ronda. But we need to talk,' he says.

'You could have phoned me first,' I grumble.

'It's important, and we don't have much time.'

'I'll leave you to it.' Tina kisses me on the cheek.

'You don't have to go, Tina,' I plead with one last effort. 'I hadn't arranged to meet Hugo.'

'I'm sorry, but this is the first opportunity I've had, Ronda. I must speak to you before tomorrow,' Hugo insists.

'That's fine, Ronda. Call me later.' Tina squeezes my arm and waves at Hugo.

'Thanks for this.' I wave the brown bag at her, and she laughs. 'And, good luck with the outlaws!'

After she's gone, Hugo and I walk in silence for a few minutes, allowing Molly to settle down. Hugo throws her ball and then pushes his hands deeper into his pockets.

'You don't look pleased to see me,' he says.

'Why should I?'

'Are you angry with me?'

'No.'

'You sound as if you are.'

I sigh. 'I saw you in the bar with Prince Abdul.'

'Okay.'

'What do you mean, okay?'

'And you went home with him.'

'I'm a sommelier and he and Daniel are paying me very well.'

'And you're a policeman.'

He sighs. 'Exactly. It's all work, Ronda.'

'It's all work, Ronda.' I imitate a silly high voice knowing that my anger is based on him kissing me last August, only three months ago. I thought his kiss had meant something; maybe Prince Abdul feels the same way. 'Maybe the prince is in love,' I mutter.

Hugo laughs.

To my surprise, and despite myself, I join in. I am ridiculous. What claims did I have on this handsome, international detective? I'm behaving like a jealous lover as if we're in a relationship and he's been unfaithful, when all we've done is to work together. No ties, no commitments and no obligations.

'So, what do you want me to do?' I ask, still smiling.

He stops laughing and tilts his head to regard me carefully. 'Really, you'll help?'

'Yes, absolutely.'

'You'll help us?'

I smile and hook my arm through his and take comfort in his strength. 'Of course, I've been a big baby. I'm sorry. It's complicated.'

I can't explain about James again, or my terrible judgement with men, or that I've been pitching way above me, it's all far too humiliating.

Hugo grips my arm with his and I feel close to him. Suddenly it doesn't matter that he's not in love with me. Hugo is a lovely guy and I enjoy his company. He'll be a good friend – hopefully.

'It's crucial, Ronda.'

'Okay. I'm ready.'

'I want you to stay away. Call Daniel tonight and say you have a cold or you're not well and that you can't make it on Wednesday.'

I pull my arm away from his and stand glaring at him. 'You're joking?'

'No, I'm serious.'

'Why?'

Hugo shakes his head. 'I think it will be better this way.'

'Says who?'

'Me and Inspector Joachin.'

'Don't be ridiculous. It's the last week, and I intend being there.'

Hugo shakes his head. 'No, Ronda.'

'Then tell me why.'

'I need you to trust me on this one.'

'Look, I know a lot about what's going on. I know all about James's project with this Internet currency, and he showed me the eight cheques. He's got $300, 000 from each of them – including Daniel Clarkson – who has just lost his TV contract. He's told them he could quadruple their money and because he knows a little bit about software he's blagged them into believing in him. He's a conman.'

Hugo picks up the ball for Molly.

'We don't want you there. It might be dangerous.'

'Dangerous? Do you think I'm afraid of James? I didn't spend ten years in the army, didn't fight in areas of conflict, to turn out to be frightened of a thieving rat like him.'

'I didn't say you are frightened.'

'Well, then forget your stupid idea. I'm going and that's the end of it.'

'Why are you so persistent?'

'Why? I'll tell you why, because James stole fifty grand from me and he's not getting away with it. Now, I finally have the opportunity to get back what is rightfully mine.'

'He's not going to bring cash for you tomorrow.'

'Well, maybe not. But I'll corner him somehow.'

'That's precisely why I don't want you there.'

'You think I'll mess up?'

'No, but you're coming at it from a different angle. You have a personal vendetta.'

'So?'

'It can't interfere with our plans and what we're doing. We have to sort this out, Ronda. It will be the last time they are all together.'

'And what about my money? Are you going to let him get away with it?'

'No. We will sort it out.'

'No, you won't. James will get away. He'll disappear, just like he always does – this is my last chance too.'

Hugo shakes his head, and I say earnestly, 'He will. He'll vanish just like the Russian doctor, the Crypto Queen, and he'll take everyone's money with him, and he'll live happily ever after on some remote island in the Caribbean with a harem full of women.'

'He won't. Not this time. He is in way over his head.'

'I want my money and I'm going to get it.'

Hugo shakes his head. His eyes are sad and serious.

I say, 'What do you want me to do, go to the local police?'

Hugo looks surprised. 'No, Ronda. I'm asking you to stay away. Stay out of it. Don't go or I'll—'

'Just you try stopping me.' I stand glaring at him. 'You won't win.'

\* \* \*

We're at the edge of the park, glaring at each other, and a stranger kneels to pat Molly. I walk away from Hugo, relieved to get away from him.

'Molly, come here.' I pull out her lead from my pocket.

How dare he? I will go.

Daniel and James want me there, and I'm being well paid. Also, I need the money. Besides, what's the big deal? If I had agreed to work for Inspector Joachin, they'd soon be singing a different tune, wouldn't they?

Molly sits obediently.

I clip on her lead.

The stranger in the black coat looks up; he has deep brown eyes, and I gasp. Inspector Joachin Garcia Abascal smiles at me. 'Hello, Ronda.'

'What do you want?' I say by way of greeting.

'We need to talk.'

'Are you going to give me a lethal injection if I don't agree with you?'

Inspector Joachim regards me thoughtfully and then laughs. 'Of course not.'

'Well then, I've already told Hugo I'm catering, and I'm not about to change my mind. Come on, Molly.'

'Wait, Ronda. Give me a chance to explain.'

I pause, conscious that Hugo has now caught up with us.

'Let's take a walk.' Inspector Joachin beckons me to follow him.

'I've just had a walk. Molly and I are going home.'

'Will you make us coffee and I'll tell you everything?' Inspector Joachin has a presence about him that is gentle yet strong. He has resolve, yet he's not forceful. He's not intimidating. He's the sort of guy you want on your side – just like Hugo.

127

They both stand waiting, and it's cold. Even Hugo's nose is turning pink, and I assume Inspector Joachin has climbed out of a warm car.

'Come on then,' I say grudgingly. 'Let's get this over with quickly. But I'm telling you now. I'm not changing my mind. I'm getting my money out of James, and you're not going to stop me.'

* * *

It's strange to have these two men in my flat. They're both well built, but they don't tower over me, nor do they take up all the space as some men would do. They're very respectful. They insist on taking off their wet shoes at the door and they hang their coats on the stand, before following me into the kitchen.

Molly appears happy. She finds her soft toy, a pink pig, and curls up on her bed to watch.

I throw the brown package that Tina gave me on the side and indicate for them to sit at the kitchen table while I take off my coat and prepare fresh coffee. It's not long before it's percolated and I place it on the table.

I pull out a tin with some cheese scones I'd made yesterday.

'Thank you, Ronda.' Inspector Joachin's eyes crinkle as he speaks and I imagine him at home with his wife, polite, gentle and kind. 'These look delicious.'

Beside him, Hugo is quiet. He wears blue jeans and a tight grey hoodie that shows off his muscles and broad chest. He takes a mug of coffee gratefully and blows on it before sipping slowly.

'I know that Hugo told you about Enrique Suarez. We had been monitoring him, thinking he was involved in trafficking black market goods, like a pair of pearl earrings that we assumed would fund an international drugs cartel in Eastern Europe. But instead, to our surprise and as Hugo told you, he came to England. By coincidence, over the past few years, Hugo has worked as a sommelier for Prince Abdul. Therefore he was trusted to work at Daniel's pub in Kent for this secret, private meeting.'

I look at Hugo, who focuses on the dark liquid in his mug. I wonder how much Inspector Joachin knows about Hugo's relationship with the prince, but I say nothing.

Inspector Joachin continues. 'The first meeting, two weeks ago, was an eye-opener and the people invited to the secret meeting were specifically chosen; celebrities, billionaires, a prince, a lord – all people of influence. People that we knew of, but who we never expected to meet together en masse. Even more surprising was James Frampton. We had no idea who he was at all. There was no record or file on him anywhere.'

Inspector Joachin eats the scone slowly and pauses to finish a mouthful before continuing.

'Obviously, Hugo was in a prime position, as a sommelier, to listen to everything and to understand what was happening. At the first meeting, James pitched his idea to his guests. He sounded them out. He's a good salesman and he explained the project well. Afterwards, you can imagine, we had to find out what was going on, and if the INTmon was a legitimate business, a proper and legal set-up. Remember, Ronda, the banks are used to controlling money. If a group of business people get together and take over the financial arm of the Internet, it could affect them very badly. The problem with digital currencies is that there's no central body to control it. As you probably know, banks provide the money in circulation, but they're underwritten with gold. INTmon is not backed by any solid asset.'

I sip my coffee.

How had James done this?

'Over the last couple of weeks, we've had to do a lot of digging and a massive amount of research, to make sure that we don't make fools of ourselves, and also to make sure we don't upset ongoing investigations by more senior forces.'

'He means the FBI or the CIA,' Hugo explains, looking at me for the first time.

Inspector Joachin nods. 'That's right, and the thing is, we've found nothing. No other police or investigating force knows anything, which is highly unusual, but that's because it's all been done on a 'need to know' basis and only a handful of people are involved.'

Inspector Joachin raises his mug to his lips, and it's Hugo who continues.

'We had to find out who James was. Where or how could he come up with the software to control the financial transactions? We also looked into INTmon as a limited company, and we managed to trace the company through many false and fake identities, bogus business names, offshore accounts, shell companies – around the world – to find the shareholders. We need to know who is masterminding it all.'

'Well, it wouldn't be James.' I refill our coffee. 'He's never had these contacts. He's never known or mixed with any of these celebrities.'

'Exactly.' Hugo sits back in his chair.

Inspector Joachin continues, 'James is the frontman. He's the puppet. He's the showman. But it isn't all his idea.'

I exhale loudly, and my shoulders slump. 'Thank goodness.'

'Why do you say that?'

'I had this awful feeling that I'd underestimated him in the two years we were together. I realised he was a talker, a bullshitter and he liked the good life. So, in a way, I'm pleased I'm right. I'd have hated it if he'd been cleverer than I thought.'

Inspector Joachin smiles. 'He's clever. But he's not intelligent. Therein lies the difference.'

I nod. 'So, who *is* behind it all?'

I hold my breath.

Inspector Joachin looks at his wedding ring. He twists it around his finger. 'We're not sure, but one thing is certain, all the investors invited to the lunch have been chosen for a specific reason.'

'All of them?' I ask.

Hugo nods, to support his boss. 'Including James.'

# 11

# Chapter 11

*'Before the widespread rise of the Internet and easy publishing tools, influence was largely in the hands of those who could reach the widest audience, the people with printing presses or access to a wide audience on television or radio, all one-way mediums that concentrated power in the hands of the few.'*
**Matt Mullenweg**

I look out of the window onto the small patio. Rain is falling heavily, splashing against the glass, and I switch on a light.

'I'm not sure if I want to hear any more,' I say.

I can walk away. I can leave them to deal with it and I can stay at home. They will find out the truth. I trust them.

Do I need to get involved?

'We can leave it at that, Ronda,' says Inspector Joachin.

'But then you'll still ask me not to go, won't you?'

'Yes.'

'And if I refuse?'

Inspector Joachin replies quietly, 'I don't want to do it, but I'll have the police pick you up and keep you in custody until this is over.'

I turn from the window. 'At least you're honest with me.'

'You must trust us.' Hugo leans his arms on the table.

I sit down opposite him and say quietly, 'I want my money back, and I'll do whatever it takes. Now, last August you asked me to work for you and I turned you down. But now I'm in. Let me go and cater for the group one last time. Let me do what I do best. I'll be your eyes and your ears and I'll stay out of trouble.'

Hugo looks at Inspector Joachin, who turns his wedding ring thoughtfully.

'I mean, come on.' I laugh. 'Who else have you got on the inside? Don't tell me Billy or Daisy are undercover police.'

Hugo shakes his head and smiles. 'No, they're legit catering staff from the pub.'

'Right, so then you need me. Hugo will be in the dining room and I'll be covering the kitchen. What can go wrong?'

Inspector Joachin inhales deeply, his brow furrows into a crease, and he hesitates.

'Well?' I insist.

'It's not as simple as that, Ronda. We don't know what to expect this time. It's going to be different.'

'In what way?'

'We believe the masterminds will reveal themselves.' Inspector Joachin finishes his coffee. 'James has formed this initial group of investors – influencers – as the core of the inner sanctum. He's told them they will know the truth. It's all about trust, and although the people who are behind the scheme want to remain anonymous to the public, they are prepared to meet this group of influencers.'

'Why are they revealing themselves if they want to remain

anonymous?' I ask.

'Because Aiden Moore insisted. He told James he wasn't investing in people he didn't know. He refused to put money into a project that wasn't open and upfront. Then the others started to pull out and James panicked. He got nervous.'

'Is that why he gave the wine to Prince Abdul?' I ask Hugo. He nods.

Inspector Joachin raises his hand. 'James made a promise to them all that the two directors would both show up.'

'So they are definitely both coming?'

Hugo shrugs. 'We don't know for sure, but James seems to think so.'

'But that's what you want, isn't it? Don't you want to know who the people are at the top?'

'Of course, but we imagine security will be tight.' Inspector Joachin looks grim.

'Do you have any idea who they are?' I ask.

'No, and James is cautious. His messages are all scrambled so we can't access them or trace the calls.'

'How annoying.' I smile. 'Then you need me there, as a backup. Just in case—'

'No.' Hugo shakes his head. 'Definitely not. You're too emotionally involved and you have a different agenda than us.'

'Just because I want my money, doesn't mean that I can't be professional. I'm a trained soldier, remember? That's why you came to me in the first place.'

'No. We came to you because you are a chef and you were employed by a man we were watching.'

'But I'm not an ordinary civilian. You know I have all the relevant skills.'

'You left the army four years ago.' Hugo bangs his fist on the table.

'Three—'

'It doesn't matter.'

Inspector Joaquin holds up a hand between us.

'She's right, Hugo. Let's not mess around any longer. If Ronda is in, then it will be easier than trying to substitute her at this late stage. Besides, it might make James, and Daniel, uneasy if she's not there.'

Hugo turns down the corners of his mouth. He's not happy, so I smile sweetly at him. He stands up, and I reach out and cover his hand with mine.

'Wait, Hugo. You're not going anywhere. You said this group were all there for a reason and, if I'm in, then I need to know why. It would be best if you filled me in on everything. No secrets.'

Hugo is clearly exasperated and he looks at Inspector Joachin for support, but to my delight, the inspector grins and says, 'You've won, Ronda. You've won the battle. We'll tell you everything we know.'

\* \* \*

'They all have a secret.' Hugo leans back and folds his arms while I make fresh coffee. I produce a fruit cake I'd made earlier this morning, to give Tina for looking after Molly, so I place it on the table and cut a large slice each for the men. She'll understand why a few pieces are missing.

I notice their silent appreciation as they eat. Slowly, Hugo explains.

'As far as we can make out, James was chosen because he

does know about software. You said that yourself. He's dabbled in a few bits and pieces but nothing major. Importantly, he knows enough to understand geek speak and to impress non-technology people.'

Hugo lifts more cake into his mouth. There's a crumb stuck in the corner of his lips, and he wipes it away with a paper napkin.

'Now, we believe that James is the fall guy. You know, just in case things go wrong. He's the frontman. He's the one that everyone has met and the man who's persuaded them to invest. So if it all goes pear-shaped, they will blame him. But as you know, he's a manipulator and he likes power, he likes to be seen as the showman. So right now, he's in his element. He sees himself as a conductor and all the others are in his orchestra, performing to his tune.'

'You're so right. That's typical James. How did you find out all that?'

'I remember what you've told me about him, and of course, I'm lucky to have a working relationship with Prince Abdul. He's not a stupid man, and he has conducted some of his own investigations. He can find nothing on record against James.'

I shake my head. 'James is like a slippery eel.'

Hugo continues, 'We've looked through his employment records. We've talked to his bosses or line managers in various companies, and they've pretty much said the same thing. James is basically lazy. He steals others' ideas, and he makes them his own. He's happy to take the credit for things and quick to blame others when things go wrong. He has no morals or scruples.'

'That sounds like the James I know.'

'He's also skilful at grooming people. He's attentive, charming and he can make someone feel as if they're more important than anyone else.'

'That's true.'

'He's successfully managed to impress eight very savvy, wealthy and intelligent business people to part with a considerable sum of money.'

I shake my head, and I feel a wave of anger rising inside me.

'Now, more importantly, Ronda, we found out that he was trying to peddle a software programme similar to a blockchain and that's what interested the two directors. He told Prince Abdul that these people approached him because he had the solution for the perfect Internet currency. He believes he has built the perfect blockchain to record all the financial Internet transactions—'

'But he hasn't nailed it—' I interrupt.

Hugo nods. 'We don't know for sure.'

'He's pretending he's perfected it?'

'Probably. It's highly complex, and thousands of programmers have been trying to develop one.'

'He's such a rat,' I say.

'Well, he seems to have perfected it enough to fool those who don't know. We have people in our team looking into it, but we must be careful. We don't want to upset any plans for this week.'

'Do you think the two directors know?'

Inspector Joachin leans forward and cuts another slice of cake. 'We assume they must know and they are happy for him to continue.'

'So, the directors and James all know that they are conning this group of people?'

'We believe so, yes.'

137

'What happens when they get found out?' I ask.

Inspector Joachin shrugs. 'I guess they're planning to disappear with the investment money before that happens.'

I sigh and sit back in the chair. Molly looks hopefully at me and stretches.

'Okay, so what about the others in the group. What are their secrets?'

'Daniel Clarkson is on the verge of bankruptcy. His wife is taking him to court. It looks like his pub might go into liquidation.' Inspector Joachin pauses. 'And, it also turns out his TV contract isn't being renewed.'

Hugo wipes his mouth with a paper napkin.

'Lord Bonner was cautioned a few years ago for accepting a bribe to vote for longer opening hours on Sundays. He was on the side of one of the biggest retail chains. He lost his seat in the House of Commons, but he had influence with the PM and he was bumped up to the upper chamber. He said nothing had been proved. The fact that they found a property transferred to his name in the Cotswolds, he said was a coincidence and he said he could prove he'd paid for it. We think someone was paid off along the way.'

'Wasn't he also involved in a railway scandal and a business park where he would have gained an enormous sum of money?' I ask.

'Yes,' Hugo replies. 'He's a very corrupt politician.'

'What about Enrique Suarez? Weren't you suspicious of him already?'

'He first came to our attention from a journalistic piece which he published in *El País*. He wrote that he'd helped his wife through depression until her suicide, but it was the opposite; he pushed her to it. She couldn't stand the shame. He was corrupt

– involved in the black market – and after he purchased a rare and valuable necklace she went to the police, but they didn't believe her. She thought no one would ever believe her. She killed herself four months ago.'

'How awful.'

'It was the wife's sister who suspected Enrique, and she has been working closely with us to put him behind bars.'

'He doesn't look like an unhappy widower.'

I offer them more cake, but they shake their heads.

'Nina King's secret is that she is addicted to cosmetic surgery. She needs more money to satisfy her cravings.' Inspector Joachin pushes his mug forward for a refill. 'And Aiden Moore thinks this investment might save him, but he's cautious. He's had some very dodgy advice from a corrupt accountant who has ripped him off, and given him bad advice about offshore tax evasion. The accountant was caught and will go to prison although he maintains he's innocent, but Aiden Moore has lost a vast amount of his wealth. He is one of the youngest billionaires.'

'Poor Aiden. I like him. And Gloria, please don't tell me she isn't as perfect as she seems.'

'She's a secret gambler.' Hugo grins. 'Don't tell Daisy.'

'Oh, goodness.'

'She's lost over fifteen million dollars recently, mostly through casinos. She loves betting on the horses but she's made a lot of bad investments, including the purchase of a dog-racing track, back in Canada. She's doing this European tour to pay off her debts. But since she's been in France, she's travelled to Monte Carlo and lost a fortune on the roulette wheel.'

'I can't believe it.' I shake my head. 'The secrets of the rich and famous.'

'Then, there is Prakash Khan. He has two wives. He maintains two families, one in England and one in India. They know nothing about each other.'

This time it's my turn to laugh. 'He doesn't look the type. He seems such a gentleman.'

Hugo smiles. 'He's very low profile. He never does interviews or meets journalists. He stays firmly in the background and for a very good reason.'

'And, lastly.' I sigh and stare at Hugo. 'Finally, what about the handsome prince with the sleepy eyes? Let me guess. I imagine that Prince Abdul is gay and his family don't know.'

It's Inspector Joachin who answers while Hugo stirs his coffee.

'They don't want to know. If he was caught, goodness knows what they would do to him. Homosexuality is banned in the Middle East. It wouldn't be pleasant.'

Even though I'm staring at Hugo, he won't look at me.

Inspector Joachin seems oblivious of their relationship, but it wouldn't be the first time that an undercover cop has fallen in love inappropriately.

* * *

'So, let me get this right,' I say. 'This group have all been invited to invest in INTmon because they have a secret and because they are influencers on social media and will encourage others to invest in the scheme.'

Inspector Joachin glances at his watch and speaks with more urgency as if he's in a hurry. Then he ticks off the people on his fingers.

'James is the showman who will take the rap if things go

wrong. Lord Bonner is in a position to lobby for permissions and to keep the banks off their back. Enrique Suarez is an influencer in Europe, Nina King has followers mostly in the UK, Russia and northern Europe. Aiden Moore is influential in America. Gloria, as you know, is global, including Japan and China. Prakash Khan has business empires in India and the Fast East, and Prince Abdul spends some of his time in the Middle East but is responsible for his father's investments in South America. This is a global Internet currency; they will lead by example using this currency for transactions in their various businesses and industries around the world.'

My kitchen falls silent. Only Molly stretches and yawns, then after walking in tiny circles settles comfortably again on her bed.

'It's massive,' I whisper.

'More than massive,' Inspector Joachin replies. He nods at Hugo, and together they stand up.' Right, I must go, thank you, Ronda. That cake was delicious.'

I watch them pull on their coats.

'Do you want me to do anything specifically? How can I help?'

'Do nothing at the moment. But if things get difficult, then run. Hide, Ronda. There's a lot at stake and these people won't take prisoners.'

They pull on their coats. Hugo smiles politely. Inspector Joachin kisses me on both cheeks, and after I close the door behind them, I lean my back against it and sigh with relief. I hadn't realised I'd felt so tense.

Molly stares at me, then sighs heavily.

'Well, Molly. Who was the clever one then?' At the sound of her name she pricks up her ears, but she doesn't reply, so I continue, 'First of all, they didn't want me at the pub, and now I'm enlisted to help them – but they don't want me to do anything. It seems as if they want me there, but they couldn't ask me for my help because they knew I'd say no – I've already turned them down.' I pause and then lean over to pat her head, and she rolls onto her back for a tummy tickle. 'I think I've overplayed my hand, Molly. Why do I feel as though they have completely manipulated me?'

* * *

On Wednesday morning, I'm nervous. I've hardly slept, and my body is filled with tension. I make a flask of coffee to drink on the journey and set off a little ahead of schedule. Using my hands-free, I call Tina. She's getting ready for work, and our conversation is sporadic as she dresses, searching for her clothes.

'How was lunch with the outlaws?'

'They were lovely. I like them, Ronda. They were so welcoming.'

'You didn't pick up last night,' I complain. 'I wanted to speak to you.'

'Graham and I had a date night. Shit! Where's my other shoe?'

'After the walk, Hugo and Inspector Joachin came back to my flat.'

'He's fit looking, that Hugo.'

'That's not the point,' I reply tersely.

'What did they want?'

'Well, at first they didn't want me to go today, but having been awake most of the night, I've been thinking about it. I think they wanted me there, and by telling me not to go, they've enlisted my help.'

'Does that even make sense?'

'It does after a sleepless night and gallons of coffee. It's as if they wanted to enlist me, but when I said no, they figured out another way. By telling me they didn't want me there, they knew I'd insist on going. It's called reverse psychology, and it puts me squarely in their camp. I even offered to help.'

Tina laughs. 'They know you so well. I don't think you can stay out of trouble, can you?'

'It's frightening how well they know me,' I agree. 'But I don't go looking for trouble, Tina. It seems to follow me around.'

'So, what do you have to do today?'

'Keep alert, and report back on any conversations or things I see after it's all over. I guess there will be a debriefing session tomorrow.'

'Have they called the local police or got anyone else involved?'

'Like who?'

'Well, if it's such a big scam they could have involved the FBI or MI5, the Flying Squad.'

'I don't think it will come to that. It's a meeting, a scam, there won't be trouble or anything.'

'Christ! You really are a crap detective, Ronda.'

'I'm not a detective. I'm a world-class chef, remember?'

'Have you got your knives with you?'

'Of course.'

'Well don't use them on James. I don't want you going to prison.'

\* \* \*

I drive through the sleepy Kent village with the thatched roofs, gabled cottages and quaint road signs and, where bedroom curtains are still drawn, people are sleeping. I park outside The Cockerel and the Guinea Pig and wait.

Today, it looks different.

There is no welcoming smoke rising from the chimney, and instead of it looking warm, cosy and inviting, the pub seems forlorn and cold as if the soul has left, like a thief in the night.

I shiver and step out of the car. It's damp and misty, but there's something melancholy about the countryside, and I pause for a while to look across the deserted fields, and toward the place where Gloria's helicopter landed two weeks ago.

There's a white van parked beside Daniel's Porsche Cayenne, and I assume it's the men who are sweeping the place again for bugs or recording devices. I pull out my bag and wander in through the back door.

Inside the kitchen it's warm and, unlike my first visit, there's no welcoming smell of percolating coffee. Instead, there are two men in dark trousers and shirts who are each holding an Alsatian on a lead, checking the cupboards, the pantry and even the fridges; sniffing, smelling scents.

I stand with my hand on the back door handle, and Daniel turns around and appears surprised to see me. He's dressed in casual jeans and a chequered shirt. He hasn't shaved yet.

I pause. 'Morning.'

'Come in, come in. They don't bite.' Daniel grins.

I close the door. 'What's going on?' I ask.

The two men allow the dogs to sniff me and, without speaking, they walk the dogs away toward the bar. It's obvious that they have a specific route, and that they're focused and trained.

Daniel grins apologetically. 'It wasn't my idea, Ronda. James sent them.'

I toss my bag onto the counter and face him. It all seems different today. The kitchen is colder, and there's an atmosphere I can't identify, but I can see that Daniel is nervous. He glances periodically in the direction of the men.

He whispers, 'I don't think they want me following them but I want to keep an eye out.'

'Of course.'

'Coffee?' he says with false optimism. Usually, the water has been prepared and Daniel is in charge, but now he's floundering.

Is he shaking?

'Do you want me to make it, Daniel?'

He smiles gratefully. 'Thank you, Ronda. They shouldn't be long, but they want to go down into the cellar and I—'

'Look, leave that. Go and sort them out, then we can relax and plan the day and menus.' I grin.

'Thanks. You're an absolute star.'

While he's gone, I look at the three large trays laid out on the counter and begin to assess today's menus, wondering if I'm cooking for two extra people, VIPs – or more.

Daniel has excelled himself. He's bought large trays of oranges, lemons, wild berries and fresh vegetables. There's also chicken breast, ribeye beef, Spanish jamón, fresh calamari and large succulent prawns, all delivered from the local market.

It will be a busy morning.

I check through the list of tapas recipes that Daniel has left on the counter. I allocate the ingredients to the recipes, making notes for prep time and cooking time, and by the time I've finished, I have a brief timetable organised.

I glance at my watch. Daisy and Billy will be here in an hour which is just as well, as there seems to be a mountain of food to prepare.

I inspect the fruit, turning ripe blueberries in my hand and checking the strawberries for a summer Pavlova. I'm impressed. Daniel buys good produce.

Even though I'm using my craft and my catering skills, I have a sixth sense, and I'm conscious of the strangers and the sniffer dogs moving through the building.

Having catered for troops in war zones, I'm very aware of my surroundings – the feeling reminds me of my army days. It's unnerving and although I'm not frightened of them, they unsettle the ordinarily calm and tranquil atmosphere. I've worked alongside colleagues in the military and their canine partners on many occasions, and what unnerves me the most is the fact that they are here at all.

It was James's idea. Who is he protecting?

Daniel is edgy, and this has a knock-on effect on me. I take a deep breath. I hold my hand out straight, and it's not shaking. My early run and quick workout this morning have shaken off my lack of sleep, and now I am alert and tuned in.

I will not be affected by anyone. I have trained for far more difficult missions and I've worked in far more hostile environments than this one.

I straighten my shoulders and flex my fingers and limber up with a few kickboxing warm-up exercises; I squat, kick back my legs in a push-up, jump up and punch the sky, and repeat. Then I jog on the spot as I punch my fists to the sky. I'd completed my full kickboxing routine last night, refreshing my reflexes and toning my muscles.

Now I stretch, and pause, breathless, and look out at the misty hues across the fields. I have a strange premonition that all is not right. The last time this happened to me, in Afghanistan, three of my companions died.

# 12

# Chapter 12

*'Citizens have long been easily influenced by the opinions of others and sought social proof, but social media have amplified the phenomena to unprecedented heights. As digital devices permeate every aspect of our lives, it has boosted the way in which information can distort truth.'*
**Jens Martin Skibsted**

The men and the sniffer dogs are in the pub for almost an hour. I watch them through the window in their white van as they leave.

'They even searched the flat upstairs,' Daniel says. 'No corner has been left unsearched.'

'That's reassuring.' I smile.

He slides into the seat at the table and looks at me with a smile. 'Great coffee, thank you, Ronda. I'm sorry I haven't shaved yet, I'll go upstairs afterwards and shower and change.'

'Did you stay here last night?'

He nods. 'I sometimes do. I thought it would be best. I knew they'd be here early.'

'What are they looking for?' I ask innocently.

'Well, I know we've all signed the non-disclosure agreement, but I guess it's just in case anyone has let the secret out. James wants to be sure that no one is recording anything. He wanted to make sure no one has hidden any cameras anywhere. It's espionage at its highest level. Maybe they're worried someone is hiding in the kitchen,' he grins.

'Or hiding in the cellar.' I laugh.

Daniel smiles. 'That's what I'm learning to like about you, Ronda. You're an eternal optimist.'

I smile. If only he knew.

'Who's paying for all this, you know, the security, the pub, me?'

'James, of course. He's been quite particular about the details. He's a planner and he's thought of everything in great detail.'

'He is a planner,' I agree, thinking of how he contrived to meet me, and how he then used me to get connections and eventually steal my money. 'Even down to each of the menus.' Daniel sips his coffee. 'He's very particular about his food. He always has been.'

'How did you meet him?' I ask.

Daniel frowns. 'It was about a year ago. He was at the film studios one day. In fact, I think he might have been looking for you—'

'Me?'

Daniel shrugs. 'Maybe, when I look back on it. I thought he was waiting for someone.'

I shake my head. It wasn't me.

'Oh, well, I can't remember, Ronda but he seemed very well connected. We chatted briefly, and then I bumped into him at a friend's party a few weeks later. We got talking, and he knew about The Cockerel and The Guinea Pig. He'd actually eaten here and by coincidence, he had a dinner reservation the following week.'

'Do you remember who he came with?' My mind is whirling, I was dating James a year ago, and I know nothing about this.

'I think ...' Daniel pauses and I find his expression annoying. 'Actually, I remember now. It was Nina. He was looking for Nina at the film studio, and then they came here for dinner the following week.' Daniel smiles triumphantly as if he's won first prize in the school play, but I feel my anger escalating.

James had never mentioned he'd been to the film studios or this pub, or that he even knew Nina.

'So, you know James quite well then?' I probe, feeding my anger.

'So, so.' He levels his hand in an undulating manner.

'Enough to trust him?'

Daniel frowns. 'Well, obviously that's different. It's business. Besides, it's not just him. It's the whole project. Look at who he has on board. And, it really does make sense. He's done his research, and he knows what he's doing.'

He hesitates so I say, 'Sorry, I shouldn't ask you about it.'

'That's alright, Ronda. I understand. It's hard to be so close, working in the kitchen and knowing something big is going on, and I suppose, even working for people who have so much money and influence. You'd probably like to be like us?'

'Oh, that will never happen.' I smile, and when he beams back at me, I know he's missed the irony in my voice. I cup my mug in my hands. 'Do you feel excited about today?'

Daniel shakes his head. 'To be honest, I'm as nervous as anything.'

'Why?'

'Well, James said that the two special guests today are very particular. The directors of the project are crazy about security and very secretive. The last thing he wants is the paparazzi getting wind of his idea or the celebs involved and it all going crazy. He wants everything low key and he's determined to make it all go well. He's come so far—'

'And, you have no idea who these directors are?'

'None but they seem to have a handle on everything. They know what they want.'

'Including the menu.'

'Including everything.' He frowns. 'Security mostly. They're surrounded in secrecy.'

'Why did they pick here?'

Daniel sighs. 'I guess because of the investment – the project – it's very specific, and only a handful of us have been especially chosen to invest at this early stage. It makes sense, and when James mentioned this meeting to me, I knew this was the perfect place. We're out in the country. There's the field to land a chopper in and, of course, the culinary status of the pub.'

'Do you know why he chose these particular eight people?'

'Of course, they're all very wealthy, and they're influencers.'

Daniel's ego knows no bounds. He's completely unaware of the real reasons, the ones that Inspector Joachin told me about yesterday, that all of the investors have a secret.

Does James know all their secrets, or is it a coincidence?

'I can't tell you how thrilling all this is, Ronda. It's an exciting and very adventurous project and one that will take the world by storm. It's a privilege to be—'

I hold up the palm of my hand and smile.

'Don't tell me any more, Daniel, or you'll have to shoot me.'

He nods, leans back in his chair and takes a deep breath.

'Well, you'll find out soon enough, Ronda. It will be all on the news next week – maybe even by Friday. Things will move very fast. Everything is in place, and as soon as we get the go-ahead, which will probably be later today, there will be a massive campaign.'

'Really, as quickly as Friday?'

Daniel nods. 'The cheques will have cleared by now and everyone's invested – the whole group – all eight of us. The only way is up now. It's going to spiral so fast. We'll make good money and a substantial return on our investment in a relatively short time.'

'Is that what it's all about, money?'

'Well, I suppose so, but it's also our reputation on the line. We'll be recommending this new product and it's incredible, Ronda. It will change the face of the Internet and it will stop the giants at the top from controlling everything.'

'Do you mean like Amazon and Facebook?'

'Yes, and Google, all of them.' He waves his arm in dismissal. 'There are core key players, Ronda, who control our lives. If it's not the government, it's the banks, and if it's not them, then it's the powers that be or even the Internet itself. Think about it. Where would we be without it? No one can imagine a world without it. It's a key player and has more influence than governments and banks. They have their own ready-made customers; clients who will use this product, as it will be easier than anything else. The Internet holds the data of billions of people worldwide, look at how Amazon has changed the lives of so many people. This investment is an opportunity, for me, to be on the frontline and to make a difference. It's an opportunity to invest from the beginning and, my wealth and status will grow with it.' He smiles.

'You seem to have made your mind up.'

He thinks he's been clever by telling me what an incredible project it is, without divulging the fact it's cyber currency. He would be shocked if he knew that I knew all about INTmon and all the investors in the scheme and how the pyramid selling structure is paramount to its success.

'So, on a pyramid scheme you will be recruiting new investors in this project and for each new investor that you recruit you will receive a portion of the subsequent fees of their investment?'

Daniel frowns.

I continue, 'And, the more people that you encourage to invest, and the more people that these people recruit pushes you up the chain, and you're promised payment for each person enrolled?'

'No, no, the money is all reinvested in company shares. I don't receive any payments like that. It's an investment.'

'So, how can you draw money against your investment?'

Daniel grins. 'I can do it at any time. I use my invested money to buy and sell on the Internet. I'll have an account, and I'll spend from it.'

'Your online account will be topped up with payments from fees you earn from each new recruit?'

'Well, yes, I suppose so.'

'And for every new recruit that each of your recruits brings in, you earn a small percentage?' I don't add that is a pyramid scheme – there's no point – he doesn't want to see it.

Daniel grins. 'Isn't it a great plan?'

'You certainly seem to have made up your mind.'

'I have, Ronda. I know this is the future. When you're facing financial ruin, you'll clutch at any straws.' He lays his mug on the table and downturns his mouth. 'I'll be honest; it's been a difficult few months.'

He doesn't appear to be a man in financial ruin, not with that expensive car outside, so I say, 'I always thought TV work was quite lucrative.'

'It is, if you don't have a greedy bitch of a wife.'

He sighs heavily and leans across the table as if he's going to tell me something deep and meaningful, perhaps even a secret.

'She's taking me for as much as she can get. She reckons this pub was all her idea, and that she designed it and renovated it on her own. She's saying she did it all without me. She says I was in London most of the time and only appeared on the occasional weekends.'

'Can you prove she's wrong?'

'No.' He shakes his head. 'That's the problem. I can't. It's my word against hers.'

Now I can understand why he needs the money. I can also understand that if his wife did refurbish and renovate the pub, she would be entitled to a large proportion of their joint wealth.

'Well, at least you have your television career.' I keep my voice sincere, and my gaze steady.

Daniel blinks. 'Haven't you heard? They're not contracting me for that series on English pubs, and the work seems to be drying up.' He pauses and stares at an invisible spot on the table. 'It's a difficult time. You know what it's like, Ronda, you've experienced it yourself. People are fickle. There are people in the industry who get tired of you and they want a change, a new face, someone younger or more well known to their audience, and sometimes they stop supporting you.'

I nod in understanding, but I can't help but wonder if it's because of his bad temper that Daisy mentioned to me.

'It's difficult.'

'Some of the younger ones don't know how to take a joke. They take everything so seriously. You have to be so politically correct these days, it's like walking through a minefield.'

As an army veteran, he has no idea of what he's just said. He must see my disproving expression.

'Right, I'd better go and shower and shave.' He stands up.

'You're right, Daniel,' I say. 'This won't do. I'll need to get organised. Daisy and Billy will be here shortly.'

'Ah, sorry, I did mean to tell you earlier.'

'What?'

'Well that's the thing, Ronda, they're not coming.'

I stare at Daniel.

'They're not coming?' I repeat. 'Why?'

He grins apologetically.

'James didn't want them here. He felt that they got in the way last week. So, it will be you and me in the kitchen. I'll be your sous-chef. I'm all yours.' He holds his arms out wide as if he wants me to embrace him when, quite frankly, I want to punch him.

* * *

When I head to the bathroom to change into my whites, I hear Daniel in the bar, speaking on the phone. He said he would help me, so I'm surprised he hasn't gone upstairs to shower.

'For heaven's SAKE!' he shouts.

I linger in the hallway, eavesdropping, then very slowly I inch my way along the wall of the nook.

He's standing with his back to the bar, and I see his profile. His jaw is rigid, and he's clenching his left fist repeatedly.

'This isn't the time. I can't speak to you now.' He's agitated and annoyed. He paces to the window. 'I'm a busy man.'

He pauses and listens.

'I really don't care, Jenny. I don't care what you DO!'

He paces to the bar.

'For fuck's sake, Jenny! I'll get it for YOU!' he shouts. 'I'm doing the biggest deal ever, so don't harass me now.'

He's pacing between the bar and the front window that overlooks the road entrance, and now he stands with his back to me. He's waving his left hand erratically, and the other hand presses the phone to his ear.

'I'll get the money for you. You can have it, yes. NEXT WEEK. It's only money. You'll get IT! You STUPID woman.'

He waves his arm and clutches his hand into a fist before thumping it against the old beam.

'Don't you DARE threaten me. If you go to the PRESS, you will get NOTHING. I will KILL you.'

He clicks off the phone.

I move quickly and dash into the bathroom. I close the door quietly behind me. Jenny, his wife, is putting him under pressure. For him to lose his wife and job, and then to potentially lose his business, is stressful and I can understand why James's project is so enticing.

* * *

I've changed into my whites, and I'm wearing a new headband with olive green, orange, and black cotton, and when I get back to the kitchen, I begin the prep work, chopping potatoes and onions. I prepare the fruit and check my timetable; working alone, the times are tighter.

Thirty minutes later, Daniel appears and pops his head around the door.

'I'll be back in a sec, and I'll come and help you, Ronda.'

'That's fine.' I barely look up at Daniel.

If he's my sous-chef today, then he's useless. I'll have to do everything.

'Can you give me your advice?' he asks from the doorway. 'Can you spare a minute? I need you to look at the dining room.'

'I thought you were going to shower?'

'I will in a minute.'

I suppress a sigh, and I lay down my santoku knife. 'Coming.'

'I want you to see if anything is different here.' He waves his arm around the dining room. 'Does it look alright to you?'

'Why are you worried?'

I move further inside the dining room casting my eye over the details, the table display of dried flowers, fresh pink and white lilies in the corner, shining glasses and cutlery, and place settings for ten people.

'I want to double-check, make sure everything is alright, Ronda.'

'Ten guests this week, that's fine.'

He nods. 'I'm not sure if we're catering for extra personnel but if we are they'll eat in the kitchen.'

'Do you mean bodyguards?'

He doesn't reply, but he places an ashtray by the window. 'I'd better put this here for Prince Abdul. He gets so annoyed if things aren't exactly in their place.'

'I suppose he's used to servants at home.'

Daniel smiles. 'Yes, and today he's only got me and Hugo to boss around.'

'Do you know Hugo well?'

157

'He came recommended by Prince Abdul. I think he's been a sommelier a few times at his parties, you know, in the Middle East or maybe it was in South America, I can't remember.' He grins. 'But they do seem very, very close.' He smiles and taps the side of his nose with his index finger.

'What do you mean?' I ask quietly.

'Well, it's not rocket science, is it? I mean, there's a lot of gay people on television. I mix with them all the time, and I've nothing against them but they are, well, quite particular. You know, attention to detail and they can be quite fussy. You can see by the way they dress.' He pulls at his shirt. 'Don't judge me, I'm going for a shower, and although I do make an effort, it's nothing like them. I can decorate this table, but they will always find fault – they're pernickety.'

'Maybe they just like things done nicely.'

'Maybe.' Daniel smirks as if he's humouring me.

I turn away and Hugo walks into the dining room wearing his dark overcoat.

'Morning, Ronda, Daniel. I was beginning to think I was the only one here today,' he says cheerfully. 'It seems unnaturally quiet today, is everything alright?'

There's no sign of recognition that he spent time with me and was inside my flat drinking coffee and eating my homemade fruit cake and scones.

'Daisy and Billy aren't working today.' I stare at him pointedly.

'So, you're alone in the kitchen?'

'Yes.'

'I'm the sous-chef today.' Daniel steps forward. 'But I haven't got around to helping yet.'

'Or showering,' I add hastily.

'Why aren't they coming in?' Hugo asks.

'I wanted to speak to you both together about all this.' Daniel looks uncomfortable before continuing, 'Daisy and Billy aren't coming in today because James insisted that there should be fewer people. The fewer, the better. I don't have to tell you how important this meeting is and he didn't want Daisy to be over-familiar with the guests and want selfies or Billy to gossip later tomorrow with our regulars.'

'They wouldn't do that,' I object.

Hugo says nothing.

'James wants it all very low key today.' Daniel pulls a list from his pocket. 'Here's the list, Ronda. I know I emailed you one earlier in the week, but there are a few changes to the tapas. It's only tapas, so it's not difficult.'

'Only tapas,' I mimic as if it's absolutely nothing to prepare thirty different dishes within a few hours and with no help.

'It's simple enough, and you and I will go down to the cellar together, Hugo. There's a special wine I ordered specifically for today that I'd like to offer them.'

Daniel's phone rings and he turns away for privacy, so I take the opportunity to head back to the kitchen. I have a lot to do and I'm disappointed that Daisy and Billy won't be here to share the workload with me.

Hugo follows. 'It's an awful lot to do on your own. I can help you, Ronda. If you need me, just say.'

'It would have been better to have known before so that I could get started, but Daniel doesn't seem with it today. He appears distracted.'

'Why?'

In the safety of the kitchen, I whisper, 'There were two men here with sniffer dogs this morning.'

Hugo removes his coat and hangs it on the stand in the corner of the kitchen. He's heard me but doesn't reply. He's wearing a black suit with a white shirt and navy bow tie and has a matching pocket-handkerchief. He toys with a pin of the Spanish flag on his lapel and then smiles reassuringly.

'There's a lot to do.'

'I'll help, Ronda. Give me time to get the wine up from the cellar.'

'Thank you.'

I check the ingredients and set to work. Tapas of stuffed mushrooms with wild rice and spinach, *patatas bravas* with aioli, serrano ham croquettes, hot garlic prawns, spicy meat-balls, chicken empanadas, Spanish potato and onion tortilla, fried calamari with cilantro, and if there's time Spanish crab cakes with roast pepper sauce. I'll make sure there's plenty of *pan con tomate* and Spanish cheeses and an olive tapenade.

During the whole morning, I barely have time to look up. Occasionally Daniel, now showered and shaved and wearing a dark grey suit, or Hugo offers to help, which I accept gratefully. They stir ingredients and hand me spices and herbs.

We work in relative silence, each one of us lost in thought. I'm wondering what the day will bring. I have a gnawing feeling in the pit of my stomach and I suspect that things will be very different by tonight.

# 13

# Chapter 13

*'I always wanted my music to influence the life you were living emotionally – with your family, your lover, your wife, and, at a certain point, with your children.'*
**Bruce Springsteen**

I take a break before the guests arrive. I head to the bathroom and then afterwards walk the long way around to the kitchen, through the bar, looking at the pub and thinking it's an excellent place for the regulars. It's empty. It's quiet and the fire now hisses and crackles. I linger for a while looking at the bar and the rows of gleaming glasses, wondering what it's like usually and how the locals may feel knowing their pub is closed for the third Wednesday in a row.

There's a rattle of glass and Hugo emerges from the recess behind the bar where the stairs lead up to Daniel's private apartment. But he comes up from the cellar, behind the bar, carrying an armful of bottles. The cellar door is open, and an interior light illuminates the wooden staircase.

He pauses and seems genuinely surprised to see me, and he

smiles.

'Hi, Ronda.'

'Hi.'

I look at the Spanish flag pin on his jacket.

I hear footsteps coming from the dining room as Daniel approaches.

I want to ask Hugo if he's wearing a wire. I want to ask if there is help nearby if we need it, but there's no time, and then I think I'm going crazy. Why would there be trouble in this sleepy village pub in Kent?

\* \* \*

I'm alone in the kitchen when the guests begin arriving. I hear the cars skid on the gravel as they park their expensive motors out of sight, at the back of the pub. Enrique Suarez's Goldwing glides to a stop, and I lean forward, pushing my face against the glass to get a better view of him dismounting the bike. He doesn't look like a widower grieving for his wife.

Daniel flitters in and out of the kitchen and I feel his tension and pressure. I want to throttle him and tell him to relax and to stay calm, but he's a bundle of nerves. Instead, I concentrate on the tasks at hand. I scramble the eggs while the onions are frying and then I dice the boiled potatoes for the tortilla.

'Hi, Ronda.' Nina appears behind me.

'Hi, Nina.'

She's dressed in a slim, tight-fitting blue and lime-green dress that emphasises her deep red-gold hair. It's a statement dress that reveals her perfect hourglass figure. Her eyes are lined heavily in black ink, and her false eyelashes blink in a smile. When she opens her thick lips, her skin stretches across her high cheekbones.

'How are you, Ronda? It smells gorgeous in here.'

'Thank you.'

'What are you making? Is that tortilla?'

'Yes. I'm making Spanish tapas.'

'How delicious.' She watches me for a few minutes before asking, 'Have you thought any more about our conversation?'

'No.' I scrape the eggs into the pan and mash the potatoes into the fried onions. She watches me, leaning with her back against the counter. I need her to move, but she stands her ground. 'Excuse me.'

Reluctantly, she moves and pulls out her phone.

'I'm going to call my agent. I'm sure he'll be interested in you. You could go global if you get an Insta account. I could—'

'Nina?' Enrique Suarez walks in through the back door. He greets her with a kiss to both cheeks, and I remember what Hugo and Inspector Joachin told me about his wife's suicide. He carries his helmet over the arm of his padded leather jacket.

'*Hola*, Ronda. Tapas, how delicious.' He looks approvingly at the kitchen counter and the array of Spanish hams and cheeses. 'We're being spoilt today. What's this? *Queso viejo*?'

'What's that?' Nina leans across the counter.'

'It's sheep's cheese that's aged for a year. That's why it goes crumbly like this.' He smiles, and he asks,' Are you going to fry those *pimientos de Padrón*?'

'Do you mean those baby green peppers?' Nina points.

I keep my voice calm.

'Of course, I'll also toss them in olive oil and sea salt.'

'Delicious.' Enrique Suarez is confident and self-assured, and I can see by the way he stands close to Nina and the way he holds her gaze for a fraction of a second too long, that he's interested in her. She either ignores him or she doesn't notice. Her attention is focused entirely on her phone, and she takes a few photos of the dishes in progress exclaiming, pointing, lifting lids, smelling and generally getting in my way. She sends text messages. 'There!' She smiles triumphantly. 'I've messaged my agent.'

'Excuse me,' I say, edging past her to get to the fridge.

'Are you two getting a cookery course from Ronda?'

James comes in smiling. He's well dressed in a striped grey suit and black shoes. He looks successful, not at all like the scruffy software developer who sat around my flat in trainers and a hoodie a year ago.

If I wasn't stressed before with Nina and Enrique, with James here, I automatically reach for my Japanese paring knife. It's lightweight in my hand and the blade is lethal.

'Come on, guys. Let's leave Ronda to crack on.'

'Ronda should do live cooking shows,' Nina says. 'I'm going to speak to my agent.'

James isn't interested. He's distracted and points to the window.

'Look, I think that's Prince Abdul in his Lamborghini arriving. Where's Gloria?'

'In the bathroom, she drove drown with me. She's tired as she's just finished her Paris concert. Now she'll begin rehearsing for her London gig in a few weeks.'

James says. 'You can't use your phone anymore. Not today.'

Nina squeals in protest.

'I mean it, Nina. Come on.' He ushers them out of the kitchen toward the bar.

'What time are our unknown guests arriving?' Enrique asks, but I don't hear James's reply. There's the whirling of a helicopter outside, coming closer, and I know it's going to land in the field. The unknown guests are arriving by helicopter.

'Where's Daniel when you bloody need him? Daniel?' James calls angrily in the hallway. 'DANIEL?'

\* \* \*

I cut generous wedges of tortilla and plate them up while I deep fry the croquettes then I check the *gambas pil pil*, tasting before adding more oil and garlic.

Everything is under control.

Hugo puts his head around the corner of the door.

'They're here,' he whispers.

'Do you know who they are yet?'

He shakes his head. 'Are you alright?'

'Fine.'

'Sorry I couldn't help you more.'

'Don't worry.'

'They're having drinks first. James is making another short presentation. He's asked me to put up the screen. I think James has gone to the helicopter,' he adds quickly.

I'm about to point to his lapel pin, but then Daniel opens the kitchen door, and Hugo disappears.

Daniel is followed closely by two security men. They wear dark suits and have closely shaved hair. The only thing to tell them apart is that the taller, broader one has a neat ginger beard. They nod at me as they scan the kitchen, then exit, then they peer outside again, getting their bearings.

I assume they are the bodyguards of the two new guests. They're professional, and when the stockier one asks Daniel about exits, he has an American accent.

Daniel explains the layout and takes them through to the bar area.

I finish off the chicken empanadas, folding them carefully into neat triangles before I place them in the oven.

Five minutes later Daniel is back, but this time, only the security guard with the beard is with him.

'They won't get in your way, Ronda, but they have to be nearby.' He places an iPad and a shoebox on the table.

My heart sinks, if they're in the kitchen, they will be aware of my every movement. I also know that under their jackets, they are armed. They are dangerous.

Daniel nods at the shoebox on the kitchen table. 'I've collected everyone's mobile phones, Ronda. Please put yours in there.'

The security guard is watching me as I walk to the sink. I wash my hands, dry them.

There's a flurry of footsteps in the hallway and then James's voice. The VIPs are here.

I take the lid off the shoebox. There's an assorted mixture of phones. I remove my iPhone from my tunic, place it inside and then I close the lid.

The security guard looks out of the kitchen door and then walks down the hallway towards the bar. Daniel follows him.

I look at the shoebox and the iPad. They must have a way of monitoring the Wi-Fi, perhaps a scanner for radio frequencies, to detect outside communication. If anyone uses any form of transmission, they will know.

I turn away.

The stockier security guard returns with a grey roll of parcel tape. He wraps it securely around the box, and without looking at me, he carries it out of the kitchen.

I don't like feeling trapped and I wonder how the other guests will feel without their phones.

* * *

I plate up the cold dishes, and while the guests in the bar are introduced to the two directors, I carry them into the dining room. There's an assortment of Spanish cheeses, tapenades, *membrilla*, sour cream, garlic, onion and cheese dips. I place them within easy reach, so they don't have to pass plates around.

Hugo has set up the screen, and he's prepared two large silver ice buckets with chilling bottles of Bollinger. James is obviously expecting a celebration.

Outside beyond the patio and the stone wall, the small red Bell helicopter is waiting. Its two rotary blades have stopped and inside, the pilot appears to be reading.

When I come out of the dining room, Gloria is entering the bathroom.

She stops with her hand on the door handle.

'Hello, Ronda.'

'Hello.' I smile and think of Daisy.

She pauses, and I wait as she walks toward me. She looks tired, but she's still glamorous. She's dressed in navy jeans and a grey cashmere jumper.

'I haven't had a chance to thank you yet for preparing such lovely lunches these last two weeks. And I'm looking forward to lunch today.' Her smile is as wide and as generous as her compliment.

'You're welcome. Thank you. It's lovely to be appreciated.'

Gloria regards me thoughtfully. 'I'm sure you are appreciated. James speaks very highly of you. He's suggested that you cater for my thirtieth next year.'

I smile.

'What do you think? Do you fancy a trip to Montreal next spring?'

'Fantastic. It would be my pleasure.'

'It would be a small private party, maybe a couple of hundred people, would that be alright?'

'Yes.' My heart is racing excitedly. Catering for Gloria could change my career.

'I'd make it worth your while, perhaps if you came for a week and then I could host a couple of smaller, more intimate dinner parties. What do you think?'

'That would be lovely.'

'That's a lovely bandana, did you make it?'

'No, my best friend makes them for me.'

'Is she a dressmaker?'

'No, she's an international criminal lawyer.' I smile.

Gloria tilts her head. She doesn't know if I'm joking so I add, 'It's her hobby.'

'Well, it's beautiful, and it suits you. It makes your green eyes very mysterious.'

'Thank you.'

She sighs. 'Well, I'd better get back to all the excitement.' Her sarcasm isn't lost on me.

I say, 'It's an exciting day, isn't it?'

She shakes her head. 'Exciting is watching your racehorse or dog come first, Ronda. It's all about winning. This is boring. It's purely an investment.'

\* \* \*

I work methodically, but I'm also listening to everyone gathering in the bar.

Daniel comes in and makes coffee for Prince Abdul. He disappears again. The kitchen door opens and closes, and I hear snatches of conversations in the bar, a flurry of laughter, deep voices, and a woman's scream of amusement.

It's frustrating. I miss Daisy and Billy. I hadn't realised how much their banter helped to pass the time. I also miss Daisy's cheerful good nature and general nosiness. For the past two Wednesdays, she's helped me learn what was happening with our guests. She'd frequently disappear to the bathroom or go outside to spy on Gloria.

I also miss their help in the kitchen.

The two security men wander in and out. They go outside, and I watch them through the window talking to Prakesh's chauffeur, the bodyguard, who was here last week. Although it is cold and there's a hint of rain the men don't wear coats as they survey the surrounding countryside, walking the fenced border down to the road.

By contrast, Lord Bonner's driver sits in the parked car away from the back door. He's not taking much notice of anything, and it appears he's playing on his phone like he's done for the past two weeks when he eventually dozes.

After the chicken empanadas are cooked, I begin to deep fry the calamari and shallow fry the *pimientos de Padrón*. I plate up the Spanish crab cakes and add parsley garnish.

I'm waiting for Daniel to give me an idea of what time the guests will be sitting down before cooking the final dishes, when the door opens.

Aiden Moore strides in looking flustered and preoccupied. He walks to the sink, looks out of the window and then looks at the kitchen table before he notices me.

'Oh, sorry, Ronda,' he drawls in an American accent, and his smile reminds me of a movie star.

I grin. 'Can I get you anything?'

'Um, a drink of water, perhaps?'

I pour a cold glass from a bottle in the fridge, and he drinks thirstily.

'Is that the back door? Can you get to the cars that way?'

'Yes.'

He seems to consider his options.

'But I think there are some security men outside,' I add.

Aiden shakes his head. He's handsome and, like Daisy says, very similar to Idris Elba. He would make a fabulous James Bond.

'Do you have a phone, Ronda? They've taken ours away.' He frowns and turns down the corners of his mouth. 'For security reasons.'

'They taped up the shoebox and they took them away,' I reply.

He shakes his head and puffs out his cheeks in a sigh.

'What's happening?' I whisper.

He leans across the kitchen counter and shakes his head.

'I can't believe it. I know the guy. I can't believe it.' He turns away. 'I know him,' he whispers.

'Who?'

'Anthony Bryant, the chairman of this new venture, this... project. He arrived by helicopter, did you see it? It's parked in the field.'

'You know him?'

'And those thugs out there, they belong to him. They're not professional bodyguards. They're henchmen. They're not to be messed with.'

'Who is he?'

'Anthony Bryant? He's of African descent, like me. Haven't you heard of him, Tony Bryant? He's an ex-basketball star and a multimedia investor. He's got a lot of businesses in Nigeria; telecoms and that sort of thing. He's bad news. He's...' Aiden rubs his hand across his forehead and whispers, 'I've got to get out of here.'

'Why?'

'He's bad, Ronda. He does bad things.'

'What sort of bad?'

Aiden shrugs. 'He's been mixed up with all sorts of things; organised crime, drug cartels and he's suspected of intimidation. If anyone says anything he doesn't like, they get hurt. It isn't good. He's powerful. He pretends he's the victim, and he plays the race card, but he's as guilty as anyone. So far, he's kept it out of the papers, but I know people, you know, certain people talk, but they can't say anything or risk their lives.'

'How do you know him?'

Aiden blinks. 'We both lived in LA. He came to me, you know the sort of thing, and he suggested we worked together. He has this idea for a charity to help black kids on the street. At first, I thought it was a great idea, to help the kids in the street gangs who'd been hooked into drugs and gang culture but then I realised he was financing them. He was the one controlling the streets through drugs. He didn't want to help them at all; he just wanted the glory and fame. Then a couple of years ago, a rival gang shot his sister and all hell broke loose. There were a lot of killings, protests and fear on the streets. I thought he'd gone back to Nigeria, but he'd gone underground, and now he's back. He's shown up here, and he's involved in this venture.

He's dangerous. He's very, very, dangerous.'

'And he's a director of this new venture?' I clarify.

'So it seems.'

'Didn't you know who the directors were?'

'James has kept it all under wraps. He's been very clever. The first week he talked about this project and it was interesting. He left us wanting more information. He dangled the opportunity before us and then gave us the deadline speech the following week – last Wednesday. He explained everything, and we had to put up the money or shut up about it all. James laid it on thick last week. He was charming, thoughtful and the perfect host. He gave us a good presentation, and we believed in him. We all gave him a cheque. He said that once they were cleared – this Wednesday– he'd introduce us to the people at the top.' Aiden shakes his head. 'But I've been played, Ronda. We've all been played. No one would want to do business with Tony Bryant in a million years. He's a gangster.'

'Who is he with? Who came with him in the helicopter?'

'Magda Bergman.'

'Who is she?'

Aiden shrugs. 'I'd say she's the brains behind this whole scheme. She seems very quiet and intellectual. James says she's an entrepreneur and has a dual business degree in business administration and engineering physics.'

'Is she American?'

'She's Swedish.'

'What will you do?'

'I want out.'

'I'm sure you can get your money back, can't you? James will give it to you.'

Aiden shakes his head. 'I think we're all in far too deep. I want to get out of here.'

The back kitchen door opens, and the two bodyguards step inside and wander to the kitchen table.

They watch Aiden drink the water.

'Thank you, Ronda.'

Aiden nods at me and holds my gaze for a few seconds before placing the empty glass on the kitchen counter. Then he turns his back on me as if all thoughts of escaping are now impossible, and he returns to the bar.

Now, I realise that Inspector Joachin and Hugo are right to be involved. This project and the opportunity to buy into this deal of cryptocurrency and the INTmon project is beginning to stink. James has sold the idea so well that Daniel doesn't realise it's a pyramid scheme, and Aiden is quite obviously fearful of the connection to Tony Bryant.

INTmon is beginning to sound like a dangerous project, and as I check over the last details of the tapas, I know I'll have to keep my wits about me.

* * *

Daniel comes into the kitchen, beaming with bonhomie. He nods at the security men.

'Right, are you ready to go, Ronda? They're all in the dining room. The stragglers are just going in now.'

He leans closer to me, so the security men sitting at the table don't hear him, and he whispers, 'All the guests are happy, and you've made the table look lovely. Thank you. Sorry I didn't do more to help.'

'That's fine, Daniel.'

I'm frying the calamari, and he stands beside me. Suddenly

there's a cry from outside, near the bar, and I freeze.

Daniel moves quickly; the security men follow him out of the kitchen.

I glance out of the windows, but I can't see anything. I lift the pan off the heat, and I venture into the hallway. There's a commotion at the far end of the bar involving Aiden and Lord Bonner.

'I'm not staying,' Aiden says.

'You must listen, hear him out.' Lord Bonner's deep voice is unmistakable. His tone reminds me of when he spoke in the House of Commons. It's measured and calm. 'There's no need to react like this, Aiden.'

'I'm not comfortable—'

James moves to stand between the two men, and he places his arm across Aiden's shoulder. I can't hear what he says, but Aiden pulls away.

'I want to leave. You can't make me stay here, James.'

Lord Bonner takes Aiden's arm. The security guards hover.

Aiden moves away from them all.

'This is ridiculous. Your secret is safe with me – your project, or whatever you want to call it. I'm not interested in this investment. It's not for me.'

James reasons with him. 'Magda is the power behind all this. Tony Bryant is only the money. He's barely involved—'

'I don't care, James. I'm not interested, but I don't want to spoil anything. You all go ahead with the rest of the lunch, and I'll leave quietly and say nothing.'

James speaks so quietly that I can't hear him.

Aiden says, 'What do you mean? You can't force me to stay here.'

There's a scuffle in the doorway. The security men step

closer.

Behind me, Enrique Suarez calls out from the dining room.

James looks up, so I duck back into the kitchen. My heart is hammering and my hands are clammy with perspiration.

How will they stop Aiden from leaving?

Five minutes later, all seems quiet in the hallway and Daniel walks into the kitchen as if nothing has happened.

'Ronda, are you ready for me to help?'

'What's happened out there? There seems to have been a commotion.'

'Nothing. Everything is fine. I'll carry everything else through. There's no need for you to come into the dining room at all.'

'Are those James's instructions?'

Daniel looks at me but doesn't smile. There is no sign of his charismatic TV personality. 'Are the calamari ready?'

# Chapter 14

*'Neither a man nor a crowd nor a nation can be trusted to act humanely or to think sanely under the influence of a great fear.'*
**Bertrand Russell**

Daniel says, 'It's nothing personal, Ronda. It's just the way that James wants to do things today. You're not needed in the dining room today.'

I shrug. 'That's fine. What about the timing? When is James's presentation, before or after dessert?'

'He decided it would be best to do it after lunch, for a change. He wants to put everyone at their ease first.'

I slide the plates across the counter to where Daniel and Hugo are waiting. They carry the hot dishes into the dining room; *gambas pil pil*, deep-fried calamari, *jamón* croquettes and *Pimientos Padrón*.

I'd imagine that James probably wants everyone to have a few drinks first, some of that exceptional wine that Hugo fetched up from the cellar.

I've made extra tortillas, so I cut off a couple of slices and carry it to the security guards in the corner of the kitchen. The smaller one sits staring at the iPad screen. The bigger one with the ginger beard is checking his phone.

I place the tortilla in front of them on the table, with two forks. I take the opportunity to look over their shoulder. My army training tells me the small one is monitoring something on his iPad. I lean exaggeratedly between them, and I realise he's assessing all of the communication. They may have taken the iPhones from the guests, but they're not taking any chances. They are monitoring the Wi-Fi. I assume they're checking to see if anyone is wearing a wire or has a secret form of communication with the outside world.

'Would you like a drink?' I ask.

They shake their heads but thank me for the food.

I need to warn Hugo, but he's in the dining room, and I can't go in there.

I'm about to leave the kitchen, but the man with the ginger beard is on his feet.

'Where are you going?'

'To the toilet.'

He nods and then follows me into the corridor, and I'm conscious of him standing outside the bathroom waiting. He's making sure I don't go anywhere else.

I mustn't let them know that I still have my phone – and that I took it back out of the shoebox before they put the tape around it. It was a risk, but I thought I'd need it for emergencies.

I must warn Hugo but would they pick up a text message?

Shall I risk it?

I sit in the cubicle thinking about the leadership courses in the army. These are the skills I trained in, but I'm rusty. And, having lost my confidence with James, I'm only now getting

177

back on my feet and regaining it.

I pull off my bandana and rub my hands through my hair. Something isn't right but how can I warn Hugo? They probably took his phone off him, so he won't get the message anyway.

I think of texting Inspector Joachin, but what do I say?

There's no emergency yet.

It's all about risk assessment.

There is no imminent danger.

I could phone Tina, but what if they catch me? Aiden is convinced that Tony Bryant isn't a good guy. I can't even Google him to find out more information.

I slip the phone back into my pocket for emergencies. I retie my bandana, wash my hands and return to the kitchen. Ginger Beard follows me.

I can only hope for the opportunity to speak to Hugo before they detect the wire on his lapel pin. And, if they do discover it, what will they do to him?

* * *

I'm busy preparing the dessert—strawberry and blueberry Pavlova, named after the famous Russian ballerina, Anna Pavlova. The meringue is light and soft inside, and the white crust is crisp. I add the strawberries and blueberries, and I'm whipping fresh cream when Prince Abdul strolls into the kitchen.

He notices the two security men sitting at the table, and scowls. He nods at me and opens the back door. He's about to step outside when the smaller security guard stands up to follow him, so Prince Abdul pauses deliberately on the step.

Prince Abdul turns around, and the security guy stops in his tracks.

'Where's Aiden Moore?' he asks. His voice is public school, perfectly educated English, and soft in tone.

The security guard doesn't reply.

Prince Abdul lights his cheroot and blows smoke into the cold air. The door is still ajar.

It's a standoff, so Prince Abdul walks outside. The security guard follows him. They pass by the window, walking towards the back of the dining room in the direction of the field where I imagine the helicopter is still parked.

When I turn back, I see that Ginger Beard is now monitoring the iPad. They're not taking any chances.

I go to the back door.

I don't care about Ginger Beard, who stands up. He's watching me as well as keeping an eye on the iPad.

Lord Bonner's chauffeur is asleep in the car. Prakesh's bodyguard is missing.

Where is he?

Where is Aiden Moore?

I close the door and return to my work station, and Ginger Beard relaxes.

I unroll my Japanese knives and sort them by order of size, wiping them so they gleam.

Ginger Beard glances out of the window. It's as if he sees something outside and he moves quickly carrying the iPad with him, going out of the back door.

Daniel appears. His cheeks are red and his mouth is set firm in an angry line.

'What's happening?' I ask him.

'It's a mess.'

'What's a mess, the meal?'

'No, the security.'

'It's like Fort Knox,' I say.

He smiles, but his mouth is tense and it doesn't reach his eyes. He's alert and wired.

'It's turning into a shit show!' he hisses angrily, thumping the counter with his balled-up fist.

'Why?'

'That bloody Aiden Moore is messing everything up.'

'Where is he?'

'He's gone.'

'Gone?' I repeat.

'Yes, oh and by the way, they want some more tortilla, Ronda. Hurry up!'

I cut the tortilla, ignoring Daniel's increasing anger.

Aiden Moore's car is still outside.

Why is Daniel lying to me?

* * *

It's quiet. The guests are eating, and apart from the hum of their voices in the dining room, nothing is happening. I prepare a small plate of tapas and slip noiselessly through to the bar.

It's empty.

The only sound is the voices from the dining room at the end of the corridor. I leave the plate of tapas on the bar counter.

I am alone.

The cellar is closed.

I take the carpeted stairs quickly upstairs to Daniel's flat above the pub. I open the wooden door cautiously and peer inside. There's a small hallway with a mahogany dresser filled with books. There are three closed doors and a fourth door open at the far end of the corridor.

Holding my breath, I slip silently inside.

From the room at the end of the corridor comes the garbled noise of a television. It's a chat show, with an audience; clapping and canned laughter. I peer through the gap in the door. There's a desk, a computer and Prakesh's bodyguard, the barrel-chested guy from last week. He is sitting in an armchair with his feet on the table. He's laughing at the television.

I back away. Daniel told me it was a one-bedroom flat. The remaining closed doors are wooden, crooked and old. They still have keyholes, so I crouch down to spy through the closed doors; a bathroom, small kitchen and finally a bedroom.

Aiden Moore is lying on the double bed with his eyes closed. He's propped up against a pillow. His hands are tied, and his mouth is covered in grey tape.

They haven't let him go. They have him tied up as a prisoner.

I leave the apartment as silently as I entered. I tiptoe down the stairs, past the entrance to the cellar and I pick up the plate of food. I sit in the window of the bar with the plate on the table in front of me.

I pick up a pimiento and pop it into my mouth. When the smaller security guard and Prince Abdul enter the pub through the front door, they both stare at me, and I wonder if Prince Abdul was encouraged to come back inside by force.

I smile back. My mouth is dry and my heart is thumping.

\* \* \*

I don't linger at the table in the bar. There's no sign of Daniel. He must be in the dining room, so I make my way quickly back to the kitchen. A few minutes later, Ginger Beard follows me.

181

I know where Aiden Moore is and that he's safe. Now, I need to finish the desserts. I pour a sweet and sticky caramel sauce over a velvety, vanilla, egg custard flan. Then I take the sweet crepes I made earlier, an Asturian recipe from the north of Spain, and fill them with local apple compote before I prepare custard and whipped cream.

Hugo appears carrying dirty plates and glasses.

I lean across the counter, and I'm about to warn him about the pin when Daniel comes in behind him.

I frown at Hugo, to give him a signal, but he doesn't look at me. He doesn't notice. He's more conscious of Daniel at his back.

'The security men have been keeping me company.' I nod pointedly at the table in the corner.

Hugo doesn't smile.

Standing with my back to the security guard, I point at Hugo's pin, and my own chest and shake my head, but Hugo doesn't see me.

Daniel busies himself at the sink, and he lingers deliberately waiting for Hugo to leave. He won't allow us to be alone.

Hugo leaves the room.

I turn around to ask Daniel, 'Is it going well?'

He shakes his head in annoyance. 'Prince Abdul is a law unto himself. He won't bloody sit still.'

'You could tie him to the chair,' I quip, thinking of Aiden upstairs.

Daniel must know that his flat is being used to hold a guest as a hostage, against his will, and this could potentially have unmitigated repercussions.

When Daniel doesn't reply I add, 'There's a different air today in the pub. I think it's because Daisy and Billy aren't here.'

'Who?' he says irritably.

'Daisy and Billy.'

'Look, Ronda, stop complaining. You're bloody well paid so get off my case. Do your bloody job and shut up!' He storms out of the kitchen.

Ginger Beard looks up from his iPad but seems unfazed.

I finish the custard and I'm plating up and decorating the dessert dishes when Daniel and Hugo return carrying empty plates.

At the same time, the smaller security man walks in through the back door and takes the iPad. They're taking turns to walk around the outside of the building. I check my watch approximately every eight minutes.

Daniel bursts in with more plates in his hands and leaves them unceremoniously on the counter.

'They're doing the presentation after the dessert,' he says aloud, and I'm not sure if he's telling the security men or me.

Hugo is a professional. He carries everything as if he's worked all his life in the hotel and catering industry; clearing the empty tapas dishes, dirty glasses and plates. He leaves them on the kitchen counter, but he won't look at me.

How can I get his attention?

Daniel would see me writing a note, and the security duo aren't missing a trick.

I prepare the last desserts and stand aside.

Ten dessert dishes are ready and waiting.

Normally Hugo or Daniel would compliment me, but neither of them says a word. They pick up dishes without speaking and the tension is palpable.

I've finished catering for the day and I'm feeling frustrated; I pull off my apron and throw the largest pot into the sink, making an almighty clatter.

* * *

I stack the dishwasher so the first load is on. I've prepared the dishes for the second load, and I'm washing pots and pans when Nina strides in flicking her red hair over her shoulder.

'Ronda, that Pavlova is absolutely delicious. You must give me the recipe.'

I smile and turn from the sink.

'I made extra flans if you'd like some?'

'I'd like to take a few home. Will Daniel mind?'

'He normally adds any of the leftovers to the pub menu the next day, but I think he'd be delighted if you took some home with you.'

'Gloria is coming back with me. She's staying the night and I'm showing her my new house in Essex.'

'Well, I'll keep them here in the kitchen until you leave. I'm sure Daniel won't mind.'

I stand with my back to the security guard.

She glances over her shoulder and nods at the door to the dining room.

'What's wrong with Daniel today? He's not on good form, is he? He's like a different man.'

I shake my head. 'He's agitated about the new people here.'

'Really?' She giggles. 'What's to be agitated about?'

'I think Daniel wants everything to be perfect.'

Nina sighs and complains, 'It's all a bit cloak and dagger isn't it? They've even taken away my phone. I don't know why. They are so paranoid about this project becoming common knowledge. It's ridiculous—'

'Everyone will know soon, won't they?'

'Of course. That's the whole point. They want it to hit the market with a bang.'

'I thought James was in charge of it all?'

She looks at me and contemplates my question. 'Well, James did give me that impression at first.'

'How did you meet him?'

'We met at a party about a year ago.'

I was with James a year ago. He never told me he'd been to any party or that he'd met Nina.

'Did he have this idea then?'

'He said he was working on something big and it would be exceptional and that he'd be looking for investors, but they had to have specific requirements.'

'Like what?'

Nina frowns. 'Contacts, influence. He was impressed with my Insta followers and the fact I'm so popular on Twitter.' She smiles. Her skin stretches.

'What are they like? You know, the two who came this morning?'

'The directors? Well, James mentioned them last week. He told us they knew their stuff, and they were experts. They are Internet gurus, especially Magda. It's her area of expertise. She writes programmes and software and stuff like that, you know...'

'I haven't seen them, so I don't know who they are,' I encourage her. 'Do you like them?'

'Well, Magda must be over fifty. She's skinnier than me, and she's got a gorgeous figure. She's clever and has a few degrees in something important, and knows all about cyber currency and things like that. And Tony, he's a basketball star,

I recognised him immediately. He was at the BAFTAs last year. He was a guest of a friend of mine. He's great fun.'

'Is he nice?'

Nina shrugs. 'He's a bit larger than life. You know the sort, he's confident and charming.'

'Is he like Aiden?'

'Well, Aiden's in a different class. Aiden's more thoughtful. Quieter.'

'Don't you think Aiden Moore looks like Idris Elba?'

She frowns and then smiles. 'Yes, now you mention it. Aiden is gorgeous, and he's very friendly. We chatted a lot last week.'

'Where is he?' I whisper.

'He left before lunch. He had to go suddenly.'

'His car is outside.'

'Really?' Nina frowns, and without waiting, she heads for the back door.

I follow her, but I pause on the step where Prince Abdul had lit his cheroot.

The security guard looks up.

Nina comes back a few minutes later.

'You're right! That's strange. He wasn't at lunch, so I don't know where he is. Where's he gone?'

'Nina,' Daniel calls from the doorway. He taps the watch on his wrist. 'The presentation is about to start. They'd like everyone back in the dining room.'

Ginger Beard stretches, then he pats his holster under his left arm and heads outside, brushing past Nina. He gives her a slight smile. The smaller security guard who is built like a heavyweight boxer stands at the table with his gaze fixed firmly on the iPad. They're very thorough.

'Nina! For God's sake, woman,' Daniel barks.

'Coming!' Nina calls out, then she turns back to me and says quietly, 'I'll come back afterwards, Ronda. I'll get the desserts from you before I leave.'

After she's gone, I turn to see the smaller security guard on his feet staring at the iPad. It's only when he starts to speak quietly that I notice he's been wearing an earpiece all the time. It was so invisible, and I didn't even see it.

'Someone's online,' he says.

\* \* \*

The security men move quickly and are now outside, and I'm alone in the kitchen when James walks in. It's the first time I've been alone with him this week. I stand at the counter near my Japanese knives.

James looks smart in his dark suit. His blond hair has been trimmed and tapered into his neck, making him look boyish but stylish. He seems intelligent, confident and, to my dismay, like a successful business person.

'Wish me luck, Ronda.'

'Why?'

'Well, this is my lucky break. This is the deal of the century.'

'You're full of shit, James.'

'You won't say that next week when I make a killing on the stock exchange.'

'You haven't even floated the company yet. Hadn't you better go? Aren't they waiting for you?'

'I have a few minutes, Magda has gone to the bathroom.'

He walks further into the kitchen.

'Are you pissed off with me because I didn't include you in the project?'

'My only regret is that I ever trusted you in the first place. It seems like you were lining up this deal when you were with me.'

'So?'

'You met Daniel and Nina last year.'

'So what?'

'You never told me you'd met them or that you came to eat here.'

'You have found out a lot. Who's been talking?'

'The truth always comes out.'

'You wouldn't have understood.'

'Try me.'

'I was working on some software, but then Tony's got some great guys. They know more about technology than you could imagine, but they needed me to pull it together.'

'You?' I laugh scornfully.

He puffs out his chest. 'Yes.'

'What about Magda? She's the brains behind it all.'

'Magda works out the logistics.'

'Do you mean the blockchain?'

'You are well informed, Ronda. How do you know about that?'

'People talk.'

He frowns. 'Daniel can't keep his mouth shut.'

'Is that why you took my money? To buy your way into this scam?'

He smiles. 'Well, I did need to look successful and to do that I needed money.'

'Why didn't you ask me for a loan or go to the bank?'

'The bank? They wouldn't touch me, but you, Ronda. You couldn't get enough of me. You practically threw your money at me.'

'That's not true and you know it.'

He laughs. 'Either way, it doesn't matter now.'

'You're despicable. I don't know what I saw in you.'

'You don't mean that, Ronda. I know you don't. I see it in your eyes all the time. You can't help yourself. You still want me. You liked how I made you feel.'

He takes a few paces closer and he leans forward, so I'm leaning back against the counter and my back arches. I feel his hardness through his trousers and smell sweet wine on his breath.

His smiling eyes are inches from mine. I remember how we had shared a bed and woken up together. It had all been a sham—a clever ploy for him to take my money.

'Why me? There are lots of other women with more money, like Nina.'

'Because you, my darling, were so easy. Daddy never loved you and you were ready, after the wave of your success with *Masterchef*. You were so lonely and you wanted someone to share it all with.'

I was lonely.

'You were so... willing, Ronda. You see that incident in Afghanistan affected you deeply. You were traumatised, but you wanted to live. You wanted to feel alive. You wanted love. You were greedy for life—'

'I can't believe I ever loved you.'

'Even now, you're gagging for it, look at you. I could have you now, but I won't. I'm a busy man.' He grins. 'Besides, Ronda, you'd better be careful. Daniel thinks you're his property now. He told me today you're ripe for the taking and he asked me what I thought. Do you know what I told him?' James's scornful laughter is near my ear. 'I said you're probably like a hooker in bed.'

I reach behind my back for my Japanese leather roll.

His voice turns husky. 'But no one will ever be like me, Ronda. No one could ever replace me. Do you know why? Because I made you feel like no one else possibly could—'

I pull out the blade and push up my sharp paring knife right under his chin. A trickle of blood appears on his neck.

'Ahhh,' he cries.

'If you move, I will rip your throat,' I hiss.

He's almost on tiptoe. His head is tilted away from me, but I know he's too scared to move. He blinks and tries to pull away, but I dig my knife further into his skin.

'RONDA!' Hugo shouts, standing in the doorway.

I pull the knife quickly away.

James puts his hand to the trickle of blood on his neck, seeping down toward his collar. He touches it and then looks at his fingers in disbelief.

'You cut me.'

I push him away and slap a tea towel in his face.

'I'm not finished with you,' he hisses.

I push my face nearer to his. 'Well, I'm waiting too, James, because I'm certainly not finished with you either.'

Hugo clears his throat.

'Excuse me, Mr Frampton. Magda is back, and they're all ready and waiting for you in the dining room.'

# 15

# Chapter 15

*'In terms of social media, I try to have my voice heard loudly in the cacophony of other influences whether from television and the Internet or social media... I want my voice to be heard in terms of the standards and values that I try to pass on to my kids.'*
**Alan Thicke**

After they've gone, I clean the knife. I wash James's blood from the blade watching it trickle down the sink with the cold water, wondering what might have happened had Hugo not intervened, and hoping I'll have the opportunity to make James pay one day.

I dry the knife, careful of its dangerous edge and place it back in the leather roll. My hands are still, and my fingers calm. I'm not shaking. I'm pleased that my instinct kicked in. My army training is still there bubbling away inside me. I haven't lost it. Only my anger is rising at the lies James tells. He's suddenly so powerful. Seeing him mix with all these people is overwhelming. He used my money to get to where he is today. He is shameless. He'd been an excellent actor. He'd been attentive and kind, yet sometimes moody and thoughtful. Now, all his diligent, hard work is paying off. Today, he wants to taunt me. He was goading me, thinking I was too weak to do anything about it.

Somehow, he met Tony and his group of technology experts, and along with Magda, they've come up with a perfect scam. A cryptocurrency, that they say will take over the Internet — INTmon. Many companies have tried and many have failed, and they've also experienced the wrath of banks and governments unwilling to relinquish their financial hold. The all-purpose, and powerful Internet with its myriad of companies all collecting personal data, recording financial transactions and algorithms to predict just about everything, is the future. James will soon be a very, very wealthy man.

I see the security men through the window. They're checking the iPad and pointing toward the back of the dining room.

I risk a walk to the bathroom where I retie my bandana and splash water on my face, and when I head back to the kitchen, Daniel is waiting for me.

'Where have you been?'

'To the bathroom. Why?'

'The security team think someone is wired up and listening in on the presentation.'

'Well, it isn't me.'

The back door opens, and Ginger Beard nods at Daniel to follow him through to the bar.

I wait in the kitchen, listening at the door. There are hushed voices in the hallway, and then the dining-room door opens quietly.

Daniel whispers.

Hugo's reply is quiet. There's a thud, and then it sounds like something is being dragged along the floor; the dining-room door opens and closes.

It all goes silent.

I peer into the corridor. I tiptoe over and listen at the dining-room door. James is excited. He's motivated and speaking enthusiastically. His presentation has begun. I hear words like; success, opportunity and investment.

Where is Hugo?

Did he go back inside the dining room?

Where are Daniel and the two security guards?

Behind me, there's a noise in the kitchen.

The back door opens slowly, and I turn quickly, unwilling to be caught spying. I move quickly to the counter and Daisy peers around the door.

'Hello, Ronda,' she whispers. She's holding her phone. 'Shush. Promise you won't tell Daniel, but this is my last chance to get a selfie with Gloria.'

\* \* \*

'Oh, my goodness, Daisy. You can't stay here. You must leave immediately.' I take her arm and usher her back toward the kitchen door.

'Why not?'

'Daniel won't be happy. He's not in a good mood as it is.'

'What's going on?'

'Nothing.'

'I saw the helicopter. It's still there. Did Gloria come in it? They'll be finished soon – it's almost three o'clock. Please don't snitch on me.'

'Daisy, you must go now.'

'Why?'

I open the back door and push her gently outside.

'Don't let anyone see you. Be careful. Look, I'll try and get a photo for you of Gloria. But you must leave – now.'

Daisy tilts her head to one side, but I insist. I push her firmly away and try to close the door. Her foot blocks me from closing it.

'Stop it. Leave. Go home, now, Daisy. It isn't safe and don't let anyone see you.'

She's unhappy with me, and she pouts sulkily.

I close the back door and turn around. Daniel is regarding me carefully.

'Who was that?'

'No one, I was getting some fresh air. I'm hot, and so I opened the door.'

He pushes past me and looks outside.

'Who were you talking to?'

'No one. What's wrong, Daniel?' I ask.

'Nothing.'

'You're on edge, and you're behaving very strangely,' I say deliberately loudly so that if Daisy can still hear me, she will know Daniel is with me. 'What's going on?'

'Ronda, stop with your questions! They'll all be gone in half an hour, and you can wash up and go home. I never want to see you again.'

He slams the back door and tries to push past me to get back to the dining room, but I'm angry with him, and I stand blocking his path.

'That's not what James said. He seems to think you'd told him I was ripe for the taking.'

Daniel stops and frowns. Then a sly embarrassed smile

covers his face, and I know what James said was true.

'It's just *boys' talk*. It didn't mean anything.' He attempts to walk past me, but I quickly pick up my paring knife and hold it toward his face.

'You may be paying me good money, Daniel Clarkson. But let's hope I never hear you speaking *boys' talk* again because it's unflattering, rude and extremely narcissistic.'

\* \* \*

After a quick and insincere apology, Daniel flees from the kitchen. I push my knife back in the leather roll and gaze at the different blades, the shapes and assortment of expensive knives. Fleetingly, I'm taken back to my days in the army in combat zones, and the fear, the adrenaline and excitement. I'm reminded of the noises; shouting, explosions, gunshots and the fear of deadly snipers.

There's a movement outside the window. I move quickly and pull open the back door.

'Daisy,' I hiss, calling her quickly. 'Are you still there?'

'Yes?' She appears instantly.

'I told you to leave.'

'I am leaving.'

'Look, be careful, there are security men all around here, and they're not very nice.'

'I will.'

'Look, if you must be here, do me a favour – go and take a look from the outside. Look into the dining room and tell me if you can see Hugo.'

'Right.' She grins.

'But be careful, Daisy.'

195

'I will.'

'Count how many people are in the room.'

'Righto.'

\* \* \*

I wait and wait. It should only take a few minutes, but when Daisy doesn't come back, I tiptoe to the dining-room door. It sounds as if the presentation is over, but there are questions and discussions. Gloria's Canadian accent is evident and sounds like a different accent to the woman replying to her. Magda's Swedish accent is stronger but her English is faultless. Their words are meaningless to me.

I haven't much time. I head back to the kitchen and pick up my paring knife and drop it into my tunic along with my mobile.

The meeting will be over soon, and they will all leave here.

Maybe they've taken Hugo upstairs with Aiden Moore, but I want to make sure Hugo is safe.

I walk quickly and quietly through the bar and I have my foot on the first step to go up to the flat when I notice the trap door to the cellar is open. The door has been pushed aside. Inside the basement is a scraping sound and then footsteps thud on the wooden staircase. Someone is coming up the cellar stairs.

I move quickly and crouch in a dark nook at the end of the bar.

Ginger Beard secures the cellar door then, using the front door of the pub, he steps outside.

I move quickly, crouching down and I unbolt the cellar door. It's in darkness. Cursing, I fumble for the light, but when I can't find it, I use my iPhone and follow the small beam down

196

the rickety wooden steps.

I pull the cellar door closed behind me and tread cautiously, scanning the dark room with my light. It's cooler down here, damp and a little musty.

Hugo is tied up.

He's propped up against a beer barrel. His hands are tied and his feet are bound at the ankles. He looks unconscious. His head is slumped forward on his chest and grey masking tape covers his mouth. There is blood dripping from his temple.

* * *

'Hugo,' I whisper, sliding quickly to kneel beside him. I tap his cheek. 'Hugo? Can you hear me?'

He opens his eyes drowsily.

I wedge the iPhone in my elbow to secure the light and pull the tape from his mouth.

'Arrgh,' he groans.

'Don't be a baby. Are you alright?' I flash the light on his wound.

'He hit me with something.'

'The handle of a gun probably. It's only a flesh wound.'

'They knew I was wired.'

'I've been trying to warn you all morning. They have an iPad that monitors the Wi-Fi, so they can see if there's a mobile or any listening or tracking devices.'

He groans.

'Are you alright? Did they hurt you?' I tug at the tape wrapped around his wrists.

'We mustn't let Tony escape,' he replies. 'If he leaves here, he'll go back to Nigeria and we won't be able to prosecute him.'

197

I pull the tape and then reach for my knife. I'm about to cut it when the cellar door opens, and we're suddenly flooded by the ceiling light.

Instinctively, I flick off my iPhone and duck away from Hugo. I crouch down behind a beer barrel, closer to the steps. My heart is beating rapidly.

Dark shoes descend the rickety stairs, but then the figure stops and crouches down. From his vantage point, the man on the stairs looks around the cellar and then his eyes rest on Hugo who has dropped his head on his chin, and he looks almost as I found him.

This man is tall, muscled and African. He fits the description of Anthony Bryant, the ex-basketball player and director of INTmon.

I hold my breath.

He turns to leave, and his steps echo on the wood. When he reaches the top, and he's back in the bar Tony Bryant says, 'He's already taken off his mouth tape. Get rid of him. Make it quick and clean.'

'Yes, Mr Bryant.'

Ginger Beard descends the stairs cautiously holding a gun with a silencer. He's a few steps from the floor when he waves the gun at the discarded tape on the floor. 'How did you get that off?'

Hugo opens his eyes and raises his head.

I launch myself forward, lunging for the barrel of his gun, taking Ginger Beard by surprise. I twist the weapon from his grip, turning my body and using my shoulder as a lever. I move under him using the bottom steps to strengthen my footing, and I heave him over my back. I smack him down onto the cement floor and the gun spins away.

He's caught off balance but recovers quickly. He reaches for me, but I duck past his arm. Instinct and years of training kick in; attack first, questions later. I spin and dropkick him in the gut, but he doesn't move. He's built of steel. He grabs my arm but with my free hand I punch him between his thighs, and he doubles over. The gun is at the floor by his feet and he reaches for it. He fires. I kick his wrist away and bring my fist down on the side of his face. He falls forward. I thump my hand down on the back of his neck and he collapses forward, so I swing my foot down and smash him in the back of the ribs.

He slumps onto the concrete, motionless.

I'm breathing hard. I take a deep breath.

My iPhone is on the floor in pieces. It's fallen from my pocket, and it's smashed. I pick up the pieces, but the battery is flattened, and the screen is cracked.

'Ronda?' Hugo whispers.

'It's fine,' I reply. 'I can tie him up.'

Hugo gasps, 'He shot me.'

'What?' I spin around. Hugo's hands are still tied, but he is gripping his thigh with his bound hands. Blood is seeping through his trousers. I move quickly, pulling off my bandana. I rip it apart to make one long bandage and use it as a tourniquet around his leg. I pull it tightly, and he grimaces. Using my knife, I rip off the tape binding his wrists and his ankles.

Hugo gasps, 'Behind you.'

I duck and spin at the same time. Ginger Beard has managed to get to his feet. He's heading for the stairs, so I hurl my knife into his back. It hits him in the shoulder, and his legs buckle. He misses the steps and stumbles. I drag him down the few steps and kick him in the back to keep him still. He's bleeding from his shoulder. I elbow him in the face before I pull his jacket down over his arms, using it to immobilise him, while I fumble to remove his shoes.

Hugo whispers, 'Are you alright, Ronda?'

I work quickly. I remove his belt and tie his hands behind his back. Then I pull off his socks. I use one to tie across his mouth and other to cover his eyes and I tie it securely behind his head.

'How did you learn to do that?' Hugo asks.

'In the army.'

He grins, but his face grimaces in pain. 'You should have joined the circus – as a knife thrower.'

'It's never too late, I suppose,' I say to Hugo. 'Keep an eye on him, and I'll be back as soon as I can.'

'Call Joachin,' he says.

'I will.'

'Aiden's disappeared,' he says.

'He's upstairs in the flat. They tied him up. Look, I have to go. The presentation is almost finished.'

Hugo reaches out for my hand. 'We need to get Tony Bryant. Don't let him leave in that helicopter. Hurry up, Ronda. Call Joachin now and be careful,' Hugo says.

I toss him the security guard's gun.

'Keep this; you never know if you might need it, especially if Tony comes down here again.'

'What about you?'

I hold up my paring knife and wipe the security guard's blood on my trousers. 'I've got a few of these in the kitchen.'

\* \* \*

I run up the stairs, and I'm about to secure the cellar door, but I turn at a sound. Daisy is watching me with big, wide open eyes.

'What's going on down there?' she asks.

'Daisy, what are you still doing here?'

'You told me to see if Hugo is in the dining room, and he isn't.'

'No, that's alright.'

I close and bolt the cellar door.

'You've left the light on down there,' she says.

'That's fine.'

'You've got blood on you.'

I glance down at my tunic and smile. 'That's normal. I'm a chef, remember?'

'It's on your hands, and you stopped cooking ages ago.'

I'm still crouching over the cellar door.

'Okay, look. I'm going to level with you, Daisy. Can you keep a secret?'

'Yes.'

'Good. Do you want to help me?'

'It depends.'

'Look, I'm one of the good guys. Me and Hugo. Do you want to be on our team?'

'Whose side is Daniel on?'

'He's not on anyone's side. He's in the middle.'

'Okay, then.'

'Right, come to the kitchen quietly, and don't say a word. I have a very important job for you.'

* * *

I've sponged Hugo's blood off my tunic and I'm washing my hands when I hear Daniel and James in the hallway. The guests are leaving the dining room. They file out towards the bar area in a sea of loud voices and excited chatter.

Nina wanders into the kitchen.

'Do you know where my phone is?' she asks.

I shake my head.

'Daniel seems to think all the phones were in here.'

I reply, 'The security guards took them. Are you leaving now? Is it all over?'

'I hope so when I get my phone.'

I begin to wrap the desserts; generous slices of Pavlova and four creamy flans.

'How did it all go?' I ask.

She shrugs. 'I think it's okay. I'm cool with it all, but Enrique isn't happy.'

'Why?'

'He doesn't believe James has the right technology, even though Tony says that he's got a full-time team working on it all.'

'And does he?'

'James says it's complicated. It's all to do with recording financial transactions. I didn't understand all that, but it sounds alright to me. They seem to know what they're doing, and if it all comes off, it will be brilliant.'

'What did Enrique say?'

'He wanted evidence of a blockchain. It's a ledger that monitors all the finances.'

'Do they have the evidence?'

'James says they do, but it's pretty impossible to prove he has until it's all launched. James insists that it's important to have trust between us all. We're investing a lot of money and we're asking all our followers to invest, so it's important that we believe in the product.'

'Trust?' I smile at the irony.

There is no limit to James's duplicity.

Behind Nina, Gloria wanders into the kitchen. She's glamorous and attractive with blue eyes and blonde hair. I do like her music, and she's as big a star as Lady Gaga, Beyoncé and Rihanna, but she's very natural and seems unaffected by her wealth and fame.

'We can go, Nina,' she says. 'The men will talk forever, but I'm exhausted.'

Nina grins at me. 'This is the first time she's travelled without her entourage.'

Gloria nudges her and smiles. 'That's not true. I'm not a diva.'

'You're not as bad as some of the celebs I've met. I'm surprised you even agreed to come down in the car with me.'

'Sometimes I need to get away and be on my own, besides it's a great way for me to see this little county. I've heard so much about Kent, and it's so hauntingly beautiful in the mist this morning. I felt inspired—'

'To write a song?' Nina asks.

Gloria replies,' I think so.' She nods at my leg. 'Is that blood on your trousers?'

I look down and see Hugo's bloody leg has seeped into my chequered trousers, so I reach for a wet cloth.

'Yes, one of the dangers of being a chef.' I smile apologetically. 'I get covered in blood.'

'And not just any chef, a *Masterchef*.'

'That blood looks—'

'What are you talking about?' Daniel strides into the kitchen. He's glaring at us, but he directs the next question at Nina. 'Who said you could talk about this?'

'About what?'

'The project.'

'We're not. I'm talking about writing a song,' Gloria says. The blood on my trousers is now hopefully forgotten.

'Besides, even if we were talking about the project. It's fine. Ronda's cool.' Nina holds out her hand to him. 'Where's my phone?'

'Ronda is NOT cool. Don't you understand, you stupid woman? This is how things get out into the public domain.'

Nina looks embarrassed and she pulls her hand back as if she's been slapped.

'There is some leftover dessert, Daniel. I thought it would be a good idea to offer it to our guests when they leave. I know that Nina would like to take some home with her, is that alright?'

My conciliatory and calm tone seems to throw Daniel.

'That's fine,' he stutters.

'Would anyone else like anything, Daniel?' I ask, trying to ignore the fact that Hugo is lying wounded in the basement with one of the bodyguards.

'Yes, Enrique wants some more Pavlova. Is there any left?'

'I made an extra one, just in case. I can bring it into the bar if you like.'

'I'll come back in two minutes.' Daniel storms out.

'Someone is pressing his buttons, isn't he wired?' Nina giggles.

'He's rude,' agrees Gloria. 'It's no wonder his wife left him.'

# 16

# Chapter 16

*'Movies can and do have tremendous influence in shaping young lives in the realm of entertainment towards the ideals and objectives of normal adulthood.'*
**Walt Disney**

I'm waiting for Daniel to come back to the kitchen, but he doesn't return. I think of Aiden upstairs in the flat guarded by Prakesh's bodyguard. Then of Hugo, with his leg bleeding and Ginger Beard tied up in the cellar.

I check the time; it's almost three-thirty and it's getting darker outside.

The dining room is empty.

I carry the Pavlova through to the bar where Gloria and Nina have joined Prakash and Prince Abdul. James is speaking to them with earnest authority, and when he makes an aside the group laugh.

James sees me carrying the dessert, and he scowls.

Enrique is sitting in the largest nook, in the middle of the bar, with a woman who I assume is Magda. She's tall, slim, fifties, with a narrow face and deep-set eyes. Tony Bryant is sitting with them. I recognise him as the man on the cellar steps who ordered Hugo to be dispatched. Now, he sits with his long arms stretched across the back of Magda's chair and his legs spread open with smug confidence.

None of them smile when I approach the table.

'Pavlova?' I look at Enrique.

He pauses his conversation. 'Thank you.'

I place it in front of him.

'It's the detail,' Enrique continues, ignoring me. 'This is what concerns me the most. What proof do we have? It hasn't been possible before, many have tried, and a blockchain is almost impossible to ...'

I walk away.

Sitting alone at another table, Lord Bonner is on the phone. How did he get his mobile? He turns his back to me and says confidentially, 'He's frightened it's a scam. One rotten apple and all that...'

\* \* \*

I'm in the dining room, clearing the table of the debris working out how I can stop Tony Bryant from leaving the pub when Daniel storms into the room. He grips the sides of my arms and spins me around to face him. His eyes are angry and his lips set in a determined line.

I control my reflexes, my urge to throw him off and punch him to the ground. I deliberately let my muscles relax, and my arms go slack at my sides.

'What do you know?' he hisses.

I frown. 'About what?'

'All of this?'

'What's all of this?'

He pushes me away and turns his back then he stands at the dining room window gazing out across the field to where the helicopter lies idle, waiting for the guests to return.

'This is a bloody nightmare.'

'What is, Daniel? I don't understand.'

He faces me and waves his arm in agitated distress.

'I don't know who to trust. You? This. All of this. It's a bloody waste of time...'

'Why?'

'Hugo was recording it all; he had a pin.'

'A pin?'

'He was recording the whole BLOODY presentation. The security guards caught him. James is furious with me. He's said he wants me out of the deal.'

'Are you sure?' Daniel looks at me as if I do not understand him, so I say, 'Are you sure Hugo was recording it, could they be mistaken?'

Daniel replies, 'It was all supposed to be so simple. What if James wants me out? What then, Ronda?'

'Go with the flow, Daniel; everything will be alright. Maybe you're overthinking?'

He scratches his head. 'It's a scam.'

'Why would it be a scam?' I whisper.

'I'm sure of it.'

'Why?'

He shakes his head.

'Do you think James is fleecing you?' I warm to the theme.

Daniel stares at me.

'I don't understand anything. Have you seen the security

men? There were two of them, and only one of them is outside now.'

I shake my head innocently. 'Where would the other one go?'

Daniel doesn't reply, and he heads toward the door.

I call out, 'The security guard isn't the only one missing, Daniel.'

He pauses and turns to me.

'I know Hugo has disappeared, but Aiden Moore wasn't at lunch either, but his car is outside. I'm getting worried and I don't think it's right.'

Daniel is at my side in a few rapid strides. He grabs my wrist and twists it firmly, burning my skin. 'Stay out of it, Ronda.'

'Ouch. Why?'

'Or you'll be the next one who goes missing.'

I want to beat him to a pulp, but I wait until he lets go of my wrist and I rub the sore skin. I want him to think he's got the upper hand, but he's unravelling. He's coming apart just like the best-laid plans. I wonder how I can work that to my advantage to stop Tony Bryant.

* * *

They are all talking in small groups. I know I don't have long. My step is light as I creep into the recess and to the stairs leading to the flat upstairs, conscious that Hugo is in the cellar below.

Inside, Prakash's bodyguard is still watching television, but now the game show has changed to snooker. I glance between the door and the frame. He's nodded off. His chin is resting on his chest and his breathing is regular.

I move swiftly. Prakash's bodyguard opens his eyes, and

although he tries to resist, one punch stuns him. I tie him up quickly, and he's trussed up like a turkey, using his belt to tie his hands and his sock wedged his mouth and the other around his eyes. Hardly a sound escapes his lips.

I tap him on the head.

'You won't be hurt if you stay quiet,' I say. 'But if Tony's bodyguards get you first, they will kill you. Do you understand?'

He nods.

'Prakash will be going home soon, and when he does, I will come and get you. Okay?'

He nods. I pat his arm.

'Trust me.'

When I open the bedroom door, Aiden is tied to the bed with his mouth still taped. He watches me enter the room in fascination. His big eyes are round and large.

I sit beside him on the bed. 'If I remove this from your mouth, promise not to make a sound?' I whisper. 'They're all downstairs in the bar, and I'm on your side. I have a plan. Okay?'

Aiden nods his head.

I pull off the tape.

'Ouch!'

'Umm, it hurts, doesn't it?'

'Who are you?' He pulls at the tape around his wrist. 'I thought you were the chef, Ronda.'

'I am, but I trained in the army for ten years.'

I pull out my knife and cut the tape around his wrists, freeing him from the iron bed frame.

Aiden balls up the tape and tosses it to one side then he pulls at the tape binding his feet.

'They can't tie me up like this. It's kidnapping.'

'I know, we can sort it, but first, I need your help.' I cut the tape easily

'To do what?'

'I have to detain Anthony Bryant, and I will need a decoy.'

'What do you mean by detain? Can't we ring for the police?'

'I've already sent for help.'

I sent Daisy off to the village half an hour ago to call Inspector Joachin. I sent her away from the pub. I didn't want her getting caught by any of the security guards using her phone.

'The police will be here soon,' I say.

'What do you want me to do?'

'Wait for five minutes, that will give me time to get back to the kitchen, and then come downstairs. They have finished their presentation and they are in the bar. This is your opportunity to confront Magda, James and Tony Bryant. They are all together. You can ask them why they did this to you. It might also be of interest to the other guests ...'

'Yes, but—'

'But what?'

'They have some very unsavoury bodyguards with them.'

'Prakash's bodyguard who was looking after you is tied up in the lounge, up here in the flat. One of the security guards is in the cellar tied up. There is one more outside, but I can deal with him.'

Aiden stares at me. 'Have you done all that?'

I nod.

'I don't know who you are, Ronda George, but that's incredible.'

I stand up. 'Right, Aiden, give me time to get back to the kitchen so that no one suspects I've helped you, then come down and cause havoc.'

He grins back at me. 'No problem, Ronda.'

\* \* \*

I make my way carefully back to the kitchen. I hear voices in the bar, but I duck down under the counter and turn the corner into the passageway and run. It's a crouching run and one that I'm familiar with since my army days. Only this time I'm not carrying the weight of all my army equipment.

My worry is Daisy.

I asked her to go back to the village and phone Inspector Joachin. I wanted to keep her out of the way and I didn't want the security men finding her. I can only assume she's finally doing as she's told and waiting for Inspector Joachin.

I glance out of the window. There's no sign of the other security guard.

I don't expect the police to arrive with sirens blazing, but it would be reassuring to know she's managed to get through to the inspector and that he's on the way.

My shoulder hurts, and I lift my tunic away to examine the skin on my shoulder; it's grazed and bruised. I move my arm in circular motions to ease the pain. Ginger Beard was tougher than he appeared.

I open the door quietly and step into the hallway to listen to the guests in the bar. They are now all in a full and frank discussion with Aiden.

'You locked me away!' he shouts.

'It was not done to harm you,' James explains calmly. 'But we didn't want you leaving and being angry. There's no need.'

'How could you do that?' asks Gloria.

'It's bizarre,' Nina adds.

Aiden is full of anger and resentment. He directs his grievances to Tony Bryant and to Magda, who seem surprised to see him at all.

Prince Abdul, who had checked for Aiden's car outside, is now standing with a smirk on his face. He's enjoying the tension and anger rising in the room. He doesn't seem to be concerned that Hugo is missing.

'This project isn't legit,' Aiden is shouting. 'It's a sham. You're ripping us off.'

'I will refund your deposit,' James says with exaggerated clarity. 'It's not a problem, Aiden.'

'It is a problem, James. You're taking everyone's money and you don't even have the blockchain developed ...'

'That's not true.'

'You are encouraging hundreds of innocent investors to part with their money in a pyramid scheme, on a global basis, to eventually float the business on the stock exchange to make millions—'

Tony replies, 'That's not illegal—'

'You want this fronted by celebrities whom you are recruiting to promote this scheme through social media.'

I step forward for a better view. James is standing with his hands held wide. He smiles at his small audience, looking for support.

'Look, let's all be sensible. I've apologised to Aiden, but I have stressed to all of you over the past three weeks that this is a unique financial opportunity. We're ahead of banks and other investors, even Facebook and Amazon. That's why this project has had to remain top secret. This is pure gold dust and I'm offering it to all of you.'

Prince Abdul lazily smokes a cheroot. Enrique Suarez occasionally nods in support, and Prakash looks bewildered as if he's astounded that anyone could doubt the project.

'You've been thorough, very professional, I'll give you that,' Aiden replies. 'You've done your homework, James. You've recruited celebrities, TV stars, a singer, entrepreneurs, a British politician.' He nods at Lord Bonner. 'And even a prince.'

Prince Abdul nods his head in acquiescence.

'But—' Aiden steps forward. 'You cannot go up against all the governments and banks. It's not possible. It won't work.'

'I think it's an incredible idea.' Prakash steps forward. 'I'm delighted to have been asked to be involved. It's brilliant technology and I think James – and Magda and Tony – have done an incredible job.'

A hush falls across the room at his endorsement. It's weighty, and I see Gloria and Nina nod in agreement.

Magda's smile is one of triumph tinged with cold disdain. Sitting beside her, with his arms and legs spread wide as if the chairs are too small for him, Tony grins and slow claps. 'Well said, Prakash.'

Tony is happy to sit back and watch the proceedings without being involved.

James is performing for them and he appears to be winning. Aiden's earlier solidarity is disintegrating and the fact he's been locked away for the past few hours seems hardly relevant now. I'd hoped they would rally against James, Magda and Tony then I could have stepped in. Together we could have overpowered them, captured Tony, and waited for the police.

I lean my head against the wall, wondering what to do next, and that's when I feel the muzzle of a silencer pressed against the back of my head.

'Don't move,' he drawls.

* * *

The small security guard pushes me back inside the kitchen using all his strength, and I lose my balance and fall against the counter. I'd never win in a fight against him.

'Where is he?'

'Who?'

He points the gun at my forehead, and I close my eyes. The smell of gun oil and the steel pressed against my skin brings back memories of my combat days, in conflict zones, mostly my two tours of Afghanistan.

'I *will* kill you,' he says.

'He's in the cellar.'

'Is there another way into the cellar apart from through the bar?'

I shake my head. 'We can ask Daniel,' I say, deliberately to delay him.

He can't look for his friend and make a fuss in full view of everyone in the bar.

The silencer digs into my skin.

'My colleague is missing. They must have a delivery chute for the kegs where the trucks can roll the beer barrels down?'

I nod.

He pushes me out of the back door ahead of him and into the cold, damp, late afternoon breeze, where the sign for The Cockerel and The Guinea Pig swings.

Natural daylight is fading.

Lord Bonner's chauffeur has woken up, and he comes out of the bushes, zipping his fly. He sees us, and I'm about to shout

214

out, but he climbs into the car without speaking.

At the side of the pub, through the windows, I glimpse the small groups in the bar. Their voices are raised. Aiden Moore is still furious. He's been untied and released from upstairs, but he's angry. He's also doing what I asked. He's causing havoc, but now I'm unable to help him.

'I've been held like a prisoner. This is disgraceful.' His voice booms from inside the bar. 'It's unacceptable, and it shows that this unholy plan – is a scam.'

The security guard pushes me in the back. 'There!'

He points to a trap door, hidden discreetly by a fence and artificial foliage. It's secured with a padlock, but when he bends over to check, the lock is open.

He keeps the gun aimed at me as he pulls on the catch and lifts the hatch.

Inside, the cellar light is still on.

As the security guard leans effortlessly and quickly inside, I'm ready to tackle him from behind. I finger the paring knife in my tunic. A swift chop to the back of his neck and he'd slump to the ground.

'It's empty,' he says, and he aims the gun at me.

'That's impossible,' I reply. How could Hugo and Ginger Beard both disappear?

He fires.

* * *

I move instinctively, my reflexes kicking in before he fires. I am lunging backwards and sideways in one swift movement. I throw my knife, and it slices his arm. He fires again and misses. He squeals when I grab his open wound, and he drops the gun into the cellar.

He's at a disadvantage, trying to regain his balance over the cellar entrance while I kick him under the chin. He falls aside, but he twists and jumps up in one swift movement taking me by surprise, and he kicks the knife from my hand. It flies across the grass. Then he jumps me. He hurls himself at me in a heavy tackle, and suddenly he's rolled over on top of me, and I'm lying on my back. Against his strength, I'll lose. His fingers dig into my eye sockets.

I bring my knee up sharply up between his legs, I wrestle from his grip, and then I head-butt him between the eyes. He falls off me, dazed. I wiggle out from under him, pushing him off me while grabbing his arm behind his back. He kneels, and I twist his hand behind his back. I could break it. He tries to stand, but I kick his calf and his leg buckles. He wheels around and smacks me across the head. I'm dizzy, but I only have one chance. I spin around and elbow him in the throat. He drops to his knees, gasping. I punch his temple and twist around to dropkick him between the shoulder blades. He tumbles down the cellar steps.

In one fluid movement, I jump down into the cellar behind him and check his pulse.

He's not moving, but he's still breathing.

I pull off my tunic and rip strips from my sleeves to tie him securely. I pull his legs up behind his back to tie to his wrists. I gag and blind him, and leave him curled on his side. He barely resists.

I check the cellar. Someone was dragged across the floor, and they left via the hatch, not the stairs to the bar. Hugo had the gun. Ginger Beard was uninjured and tied up.

Who was dragging whom?

# 17

# Chapter 17

*'Every life is a profession of faith, and exercises an inevitable and silent influence.'*
**Henri-Frédéric Amiel**

Back in the kitchen, I wash my hands and stem the bleeding on my face. The gun caught me on the cheek, and it's bruised and sore.

A voice in the kitchen behind me whispers, 'Ronda?'

I turn at the sound of my name and pick up my santoku knife. She's peering around the back door.

'Daisy, what are you doing here? I told you not to come back.'

'Oh, my goodness, you're bleeding, Ronda.'

I brush my temple with my hand. 'It's a flesh wound.'

She shakes her head. 'You're hurt as well.'

'What do you mean? As well as who?'

'You'd better come quickly.'

'What's happened?'

'It's Hugo. I think he's dying.'

\* \* \*

I follow her around the back of the pub, and we run past the expensive guests' cars, to the barbecue area at the bar near the dining room window. It's secluded here, but if anyone walked in the garden or went toward the helicopter, they'd see Hugo immediately.

He's leaning up against the stone wall, and blood has soaked his trousers. He's pale, and he seems to be drifting in and out of consciousness.

I kneel at his side. 'Hugo? Hugo?'

His head rolls forward, but he opens his eyes.

'You've lost a lot of blood. You should have stayed in the cellar.'

'I couldn't let you do this on your own.' His voice is weak, but his resolve is firm.

I pull at the tourniquet. 'It's come loose, Daisy.' I tear Hugo's trousers to see the wound. 'How did he get here?' I ask Daisy.

'I helped him.'

'When? Did you call Inspector Joachin, as I told you?'

'No. I was worried. After you left, I went straight down to the cellar.'

'You haven't been to the village?'

'No.'

'Oh, Daisy.' I'm thinking quickly. 'Did you use the outside entrance to the cellar?'

'Yes.'

So, it had been Daisy who opened the padlock. I imagine her going inside and finding Hugo bleeding and Ginger Beard tied up. She would have been in shock.

'I didn't want to leave Hugo, so I helped him up the stairs

and managed to get him outside. No one saw us.'

'What about the guy who was tied up down there?'

'We left him,' Daisy replies.

I pull off Hugo's ripped and dirty jacket and using my santoku knife, I rip it into strips.

'What's happening in the pub?' Hugo asks me.

'I released Aiden, they were holding him upstairs, and he's now creating havoc with them all.'

Hugo nods. 'And the security guys?'

'The other one is now in the cellar, and Ginger Beard is on the loose. Right, Hugo, keep alert. They're leaving soon.'

The gun is lying beside his hand on the damp grass. I edge it firmly between his fingers.

'How can we stop them?' he mumbles.

'It's Tony Bryant that you want, isn't it?'

'Yes, he's wanted by the FBI, and he's residing in Holland at the moment. If we can keep him in the UK, then they can extradite him more efficiently and put him on trial in the US.'

'Okay. I'll do my best.'

I lift Hugo's thigh and tie the material tightly around his leg.

'He needs an ambulance, urgently, Daisy. We'll never be able to do this on our own. We need to call Inspector Joachin – urgently. Where's your phone?'

Daisy pulls her phone from her pocket. Tears begin to well up in her eyes, and then they trickle down her cheeks. 'I'm so sorry, Ronda. My phone is dead.'

* * *

'Right, Daisy. Now, you must do as I say this time. Get away from here, go now. Run across the field to the village shop or someone's house and call 999. Tell them we need an ambulance urgently. You still have the number I gave you? Call Inspector Joachin. Tell him it's urgent. Tell him Tony Bryant is here and we need backup – immediately!'

I can't risk Daisy going back inside the pub.

'But what about you?' she cries.

'I'll be fine.'

She looks doubtfully at Hugo.

I say firmly, 'I'll look after him. Now go. You can save him if you run quickly.'

Daisy's fingers are shaking. She looks terrified, so I take her by the shoulders and stare into her eyes.

'Look at me,' I order. 'You're okay. You'll be fine. But you *must* go now. Don't let anyone see you.'

After she leaves, I bend down and whisper to Hugo.

'I'll be back in a few minutes. Let me see how the land lies. If you hear the helicopter start up, then you'll know Tony and Magda are leaving. You might get a clean shot at him if he runs for it. I'll try and stop him before that.'

He opens his eyes and nods.

'I've got this.' He waves the revolver and attempts a brave smile.

'Good.' I kneel and look over the stone wall, making a risk assessment of my return to the kitchen.

I can only assume Ginger Beard managed to escape. He's around here somewhere, and I imagine he's like a wounded animal; hurt, angry and with a score to settle.

* * *

Inside the kitchen, I pull a clean tunic from my bag and I tie a new colourful bandana of yellow, grey and orange around my hair, then I check my knives.

I lay out the Japanese leather roll and think quickly. I select the santoku knife and the bread knife. I wrap them in kitchen paper and place them in my tunic. I'm about to leave the kitchen when Daniel comes in.

'Where have you been?' he asks.

'The bathroom.'

'You've changed?'

'I wanted to tidy up before the guests left.'

I indicate my clean tunic, and he looks doubtful.

'I don't know why you're bothering.' Daniel slumps down at the small table and holds his face in his hands. He looks exhausted and defeated.

'Where is everyone?' I ask.

'They're in the bar. Nina and Gloria are leaving. They've had enough.'

As if on cue, Nina strolls into the kitchen.

'Ah, Ronda. Did you prepare the desserts for me to take home?'

'Of course.'

Conscious of the sharp blades in my tunic, I move cautiously, carrying the desserts to Nina's car. Gloria follows us.

'I've got a massive favour to ask.' I look at Gloria. 'There's a lovely girl, Daisy, who normally works here in the kitchen. She's been here for the past two weeks, and she'd love a photo of you.'

Gloria smiles. 'Why didn't she ask me?'

I smile and shrug as if it had never entered my head.

'I don't have my phone. Could you send her a signed picture with an autograph or something?'

'Yeah, sure. No problem.'

'Just send it here to the pub, her name is Daisy.'

'Okay.'

'You won't forget, will you?' I lean into the car.

This time the roof is up. It's almost dark, it's cold, but the heating is starting to come on, and I feel a warm gust of air.

'I'll call you,' Nina shouts from the convertible. 'And don't worry. I'll make sure Daisy gets a photo of Gloria.'

'Thank you.' I lift my arm in a wave.

'My agent will contact you.'

I wave them off and then, like Cinderella, I return to the dirty dishes in the kitchen and my role of *Masterchef*.

* * *

In the dining room, under the pretence of clearing the remaining plates and dishes, I check outside where I know Hugo is propped up against the far side of the wall, behind the barbecue. He's facing away, looking at the field where the helicopter is silhouetted in the dusky light.

I open the double dining-room doors to hear the conversation in the bar.

'This is a complete mess,' Enrique complains.

'It's a scam,' agrees Aiden. 'They kept me tied up with tape over my mouth upstairs. That's not normal.'

'You took our phones away.' Enrique joins in. 'But the ladies and Lord Bonner have got theirs back. Why?'

Ginger Beard steps forward and he has a cut on his chin. He's holding the shoebox of mobiles. He's come from the flat upstairs, and he leans forward and whispers in Tony Bryant's ear.

Tony doesn't change position, but he listens and then nods his head.

Prakash's bodyguard, who I'd tied upstairs, is now walking down the hallway toward the kitchen, and my heart begins to thump. He's another one with a grudge against me. Ginger Beard must have set him free. They are both heading toward the kitchen.

I don't want to be alone with them. I can either hide in the bathroom or head to the bar. I've never been into hiding, and besides, if this isn't sorted quickly, Hugo is likely to die.

\* \* \*

I wait until the men disappear into the kitchen and then I dash to the bar.

James raises his eyebrows and then frowns.

'What do you want, Ronda?' he asks.

Prakash, Enrique, Prince Abdul and Lord Bonner wait for me to answer.

Aiden Moore smiles and says, 'Thank goodness, here's the voice of reason. Come in, Ronda. Only Prince Abdul and Enrique seem to believe that I was tied up in the flat upstairs.'

James stands up quickly. 'This is not necessary. You can go back to the kitchen, Ronda.'

Tony stands up. He's a giant of a man. He's tall, long-limbed, and he looks much bigger as he bends his head under the low beamed ceiling.

'I think we need to adjourn. I've had enough for the day.'

'What?' James holds out his arm as if to stop him from moving. 'We can't leave it all like this. I want to reassure everyone that the project is going ahead. Aiden, I will refund your deposit – or anyone's deposit—'

'Nina and Gloria have already left. They don't want to be involved.' Aiden stands his ground.

James holds his arms wide in a gesture of innocence. 'That's not true, Aiden. They wanted to get back because it's getting dark.'

'We're going. Come on, Magda.' Tony nods his head toward the door. 'Let's get out of here. The police are involved,' he says.

'What do you mean, the police?' James objects.

Tony nods at me. 'Her.'

James points to me.

'Ronda? She's not the police.'

'She is. We're going to have to call the whole thing off.'

Tony sidesteps James's outstretched arm.

'I know for a fact that Ronda isn't police.' James blocks his path. 'She's a legitimate chef. I know for a fact because—'

'She's fooled you.' Tony shakes his head. 'You've messed up, James.'

'Ronda?' James appeals to me. 'For God's sake. Tell him you're not the police.'

'I'm not the police.' I square my shoulders. I want to take my time and keep them all here together until Daisy contacts Inspector Joachin.

Tony laughs mockingly.

'You're lying.'

James stands between us, with his back to me and facing Tony. He says calmly, 'Look, Ronda is not with the police. I used to date her for Christ's sake—'

'You what?' Enrique Suarez says.

Prince Abdul smiles.

Lord Bonner stands up. 'I agree with Tony. If the police are involved, we need to postpone everything.'

'We don't need to postpone anything.' James turns on him furiously.

'I'm with James,' Prakash nods. 'Let's go ahead. If it's out in the open anyway now—'

'It isn't out in the open,' James argues. 'It's still only us who know about the project, and it's still on target. We will launch in two days. The websites are ready to go live. The social media procedures are in place, and the money will be rolling in by Saturday.'

Daniel strolls wearily into the bar. He's dishevelled and troubled, as if he's carrying the burden of the whole thing on his shoulders. He pushes past James and looks at Tony.

'Ronda isn't police,' he announces. 'It's Hugo that we need to watch. He was the one wearing the wire.'

'What wire?' asks Prakash.

'He was recording our meeting today,' adds Daniel.

James protests. 'But it can't be Hugo. He's been here each week.'

He turns to Prince Abdul. 'You recommended him. Is Hugo undercover police?'

Prince Abdul is not smiling now. 'I've known him for years as a sommelier. I think you're very mistaken—'

Tony interrupts. 'I've had enough of this. You promised it was secure, James. I don't want any excuses.' He pulls a baseball cap out of his back pocket. 'Right, Magda. Let's go.'

'We need to make a decision,' she says. 'Is it on or not? Can we afford to wait?' She pulls herself up to her full height.

'We'll sort it out later. If James has messed up, then he will pay for it.' Tony places the cap on his head.

'I haven't messed up,' James insists. 'I knew nothing about any of this.'

'Well, that's the problem, James. You should have known. It's a good thing I brought my own security team,' Tony replies menacingly, and points at me. 'But she's tried to take them down. Let's go, Magda.'

'You kept me locked upstairs,' Aiden complains and moves to block his path. 'I'm filing a police report.'

'It was Prakash's bodyguard who did that. It's nothing to do with me.' Tony grins.

Prakash says to Tony, 'If my man is hurt in any way, I'll hold you to account. James asked if he would comply with your team this morning, and I agreed. He's followed your security team's orders. But I never realised all this was going on.'

'Whatever,' Tony shouts over his shoulder.

James moves to stop Magda from leaving, but she holds up her palms as if to ward off an evil spirit.

'Don't touch me,' she says.

'This will be alright, Magda. Let's agree to continue with our project on Friday and put this unfortunate incident behind us. We can all come together and agree to—'

Magda shakes a finger at him. 'If you've damaged all our hard work, then you will pay for it,' she hisses.

'But I haven't done anything. This is crazy.' James follows her down the corridor and I'm left looking at Lord Bonner, Enrique, Aiden and Prakash, wondering how to stop Tony from escaping while his bodyguard is still lurking in the vicinity.

# 18

# Chapter 18

*'I don't have any influences, I influence people. People watch me.'*
**Laurel Van Ness**

I run after the small group. They go through the private hallway, past the dining room to the secret entrance at the back of the pub. Tony and Magda are hurrying to the field where the helicopter is waiting. By the time I get there, James is waiting for me. He pushes me back inside and tries to close the door.

'You stupid bitch!'

He catches me off guard and hurls me against the wall and without warning, puts his arm across my throat. He punches me in the face and pushes me into the kitchen. I stumble and try to regain my footing, but he kicks my legs from under me. Suddenly, I'm grovelling on the floor. The kitchen tiles are cold on my palms and I'm on all fours as James hovers around me.

'You've wrecked it all.'

'I haven't—'

The blow with his foot hits me in my belly. I clutch my stomach, aware of the knives in my tunic.

'You didn't know I did karate, did you?' He stands with his legs apart. His hands are flat and straight. He kicks out again with his right foot, but this time I'm ready. I bat it away with my left hand as I stand and lean away from his reach, then step backwards, sending pots and pans clattering onto the floor.

James laughs and bounces on his toes.

I back away further into the kitchen.

He lunges feet first in a flying kick and he catches my shoulder. I spin away. He springs off the counter, flips around, and he's back again. Moving from side to side as if he's limbering up. Ready to fight. He clenches his fists.

'It's time I showed you the real me,' he says. He kicks out again and I brush his foot aside with my palm.

I bring my fists up to defend my face, and he laughs.

He kicks out again.

I defend.

He lashes out.

I block. I'm experienced at taking punches and I roll with them, leading him on, my confidence growing. He's an amateur; it's a sport for him, but my martial arts training has kept me alive.

I hear the whirl of the helicopter starting in the field.

'Bitch!' he says.

He leaps up, flying through the air and I pull out the carving knife from my tunic; even though it's wrapped up, it will slice him apart. He sees it mid-air and his mouth opens, but he can't stop.

I sidestep, he passes me and lands clumsily on the floor. I smack him on the back of the skull with my knife and clenched fist.

James collapses on the floor.

'You might know karate,' I whisper. 'But I've trained in Krav Maga.'

Aiden rushes in. 'Ronda, are you alright?'

He sees James lying face down on the floor and stares at me in shock.

'Wow!'

'Keep an eye on him,' I say. 'I can't let Tony get away.'

\* \* \*

The noise reminds me of Afghanistan when Apaches filled dark skies.

I race outside.

It's almost dusk and the chopper is harder to see in the fading light. My military training kicks in and I assess the situation.

The red and white Bell 206 has two rotary blades and seats up to six people. The blades are whizzing slowly around, gaining momentum, gaining rhythm for taking off.

Magda and Tony are walking quickly with Enrique at their side.

They're in discussion or even arguing, but Tony has his hand on Magda's arm. He's pulling her away toward the spinning rotors of their escape route.

Enrique appears to give up talking to them. In my peripheral vision to my right, Ginger Beard is half carrying and half dragging his colleague. He must have found him in the cellar.

Suddenly, the wail of a police siren fills the air. It's haunting in the misty fog. Then suddenly everyone is running.

Enrique runs back to the pub while Tony and Magda run to

the chopper. I chase them. The bodyguards and I are forming a triangle with the helicopter at the pinnacle.

Tony turns. He points in warning and shouts, but his words are lost in the swirling noise of the chopper's blades, firing up.

Magda sees me charging across the field. My head is down, and I'm gaining on them, but to my right, Ginger Beard drops his friend and comes running at me.

I'm winded by his rugby tackle, and I fall onto the wet grass, but roll away from his grip and spring to my feet. As he gets to his feet, I sweep kick his legs from under him. Attack is the best defence; fear is my best weapon. He topples over. I raise my foot and prepare to dropkick, but he grabs it, so I twist from his grasp, and suddenly he slumps to the grass. His knees buckle, and he falls forward. Hugo is lying in the grass, stretched out as if he's crawled on his hands and knees. He has a gun in both his hands.

The helicopter's engine is gaining momentum. Tony and Magda duck under the revolving blades and climb inside.

The smaller bodyguard is injured from our earlier fight, and now he's limping toward the helicopter.

Hugo shouts a warning.

I'll never get there in time before it takes off. I only have a few seconds before it lifts off. I run back and slide down in the grass beside Hugo.

'Give me the gun,' I shout.

I leap to my feet as the bodyguard is being pulled inside and the helicopter begins to lift off the ground. I run as the chopper rises. I aim for the fuselage. It seems futile, but I've read that a helicopter was once brought down by a spear. I won't give up. I continue walking and firing, but the chopper tilts and rises effortlessly from the ground.

The police sirens from the road come closer.

I turn around to check on Hugo, and he points at the sky.

Tony and Magda's helicopter is returning to the field. Above them, a police helicopter is guiding them down.

* * *

It lands shakily, several metres from where it took off, and as the rotary blades slow down, the door swings open. I see the bullet holes in the side of the fuselage, but I know it hasn't landed because of my shooting.

Tony climbs out, and he begins to run. This time he's not hindered by Magda. He's a professionally trained athlete, and he's still extremely fit. He runs in a loping gait back toward the pub.

I hold the revolver at my side, but it's empty. I drop it on the grass. I still have a knife tucked in my tunic, and so I pull it free and run.

I chase Tony. We're on our own, running across the field and I realise he's heading to the cars at the back of the pub.

I round the building, and I slip and fall on the gravel. Tony reaches the Bentley, pulls Lord Bonner's chauffeur from the driving seat and hurls him to the ground. He climbs in behind the steering wheel and guns the engine—the car skids and reverses on the gravel towards where I'm lying. I roll forward, reach out and I slice the back left tyre effortlessly with my Japanese blade just as Tony accelerates leaving a spew of gravel churning behind him.

I cover my eyes with my arms and spit out the dust and dirt as the car tears down the narrow lane toward the main road.

The sirens are louder, and two police cars block the entrance to the road.

Tony rams one of the police cars.

Two policemen scramble out, one speaking on the radio. Overhead the sound of a helicopter comes closer. It's not the chopper parked in the field. As I look up and shade my eyes, the lettering is very distinct: POLICE.

\* \* \*

My palms are sore and raw from the gravel. I rise to my feet and wipe the blood from my left eye. Lord Bonner's chauffeur stands beside me, and we watch the scene unfurling together. At the road entrance, the police have detained Tony Bryant. He is now sprawled across the bonnet of the police car while the two officers slip on handcuffs. Armed police are making their way up the driveway.

'Are you alright?' the chauffeur asks.

'Fine.' I turn away and call out to the officers, 'I need an ambulance urgently.'

The armed officers surround the building and run across the field to where Magda and Tony's helicopter landed, while above us another police helicopter circles.

It doesn't take long for them to move Lord Bonner's car and the ambulance crew are able to follow me around the back of the pub to the stone wall, where Hugo is lying on the grass overlooking the field where the helicopter landed, I stand aside while the medics attend to him.

Hugo opens his eyes.

'We got him.' I smile.

Hugo nods and attempts to smile through the pain.

Armed officers find the bodies of the two bodyguards lying

on the grass and I turn to watch the police escort Magda across the field, and then she's driven away quickly.

I walk beside Hugo's stretcher to the waiting ambulance. Meanwhile, I watch the medics load the two bodyguards into waiting ambulances; they're not dead, but they will need hospital treatment. They're taken away with a police escort.

The cellar doors are open, and a forensic team is already entering the premises, checking the discarded padlock and the steps. A makeshift tent is erected and equipment set up.

Inspector Joachin is standing with senior detectives at the front of the pub and he smiles when he sees me.

'They told me you were alright and you were looking after Hugo.' He looks down at Hugo and reaches for his hand.

'Well done. We'll look after you, Hugo. Get some rest.'

Hugo nods. 'Ronda was a star. Shame about her face.'

'I know.' Inspector Joachin beams at me. 'It looks sore, Ronda.'

'You should see the other guys,' I quip.

Once Hugo is inside the ambulance and the doors have closed, Inspector Joachin turns to me and says, 'There's an ambulance crew waiting to check you over, Ronda. When you've finished, I'll be inside the pub.'

It's not a request. It's an order, and twenty minutes later, my wounds are clean but my body is sore and I enter the pub through the front door for the first time.

'Where is everyone?' I ask.

Inspector Joachin replies, 'Daniel is being interviewed upstairs. Lord Bonner is in one of the nooks, and Prakash is in the other. Prince Abdul is in the dining room. Enrique Suarez is over there.' He nods at the table in the corner. 'And Aiden is outside in one of the police cars. He's told me what they did to him. And how you rescued him. They're all making statements.'

I shake my head. 'I wish I could have done more. Poor Hugo. It was an accident.'

'You'll need to make a statement.'

'Where's James?'

Inspector Joachin's eyes darken. 'They caught him trying to escape. He was aiming for the village, but Daisy saw him. The police officers picked him up.'

'Where's Daisy?'

'She's waiting for you in the kitchen.'

\* \* \*

'So, are you police?' Daisy asks. She's made tea for me and Inspector Joachin, who is busy with the detectives from the Kent Police and the National Crime Agency.

'No.'

'But these are special police, are they?'

'There are detectives and officers from the National Crime Agency. They're different to a local police force inasmuch as they are the UK's leading agency that fights organised crime; things like drugs and human trafficking. They look at the bigger picture across the UK to see how criminals operate. They're the point of contact for foreign police, and they assist police forces who may need their help.' I sip my tea. My top lip is swollen, and it burns.

'Like the Kent Police?'

'Yes.'

'Is that why they have a helicopter?'

'Probably.' I yawn. It's past seven o'clock, and I still have to give a statement and drive back to London. I also know I must phone Tina, but without my mobile, that's lying broken somewhere – it's probably still in the cellar – I don't have their telephone numbers.

Inspector Joachin has impressed Daisy, and she swoons each time he comes in and out of the kitchen.

'He's fit for an old guy,' she whispers.

'He's not old,' I whisper back.

Inspector Joachin arranges for us both to make a statement in separate areas of the dining room and when I'm finished, he's waiting for me.

'Aiden Moore has insisted on staying behind. He wants to speak to you. He's waiting in the bar.'

Aiden stands up when he sees me, and he smiles with sympathy. 'You look bruised, Ronda. You took quite a beating from those thugs. I can't believe how brave you are.'

I smile and slide into the window seat. All around us, the members of the forensic team are busy, up and down to the cellar and upstairs to the flat.

'The inspector said it was alright for me to wait here, at this table near the door.'

'You didn't have to wait.'

'I wanted to say thank you.'

'There's no need.'

'You were so incredible. I've heard so much praise for you from the inspector. He's very impressed too. He wouldn't say much, but he told me a little of your army background. I hope you don't mind.'

'That's fine. I'm honestly too tired to care.'

'Can I give you a lift home, back to London?'

I want a lift. The thought of driving back to London alone is not a welcome one, but I know it will give me time to process the events of the day.

'Thank you, Aiden, but I have my car here.'

'Right, well.' He looks unsure as the police officers move around the bar. 'Perhaps we can meet again one day?'

'I hope so.'

'You look exhausted. I won't stay now so goodbye, Ronda.'

We stand up at the same time, and he leans forward to kiss me on my sore cheek, and I flinch.

'Sorry.'

'Sorry!'

We both smile.

# Chapter 19

*'Mantovani was a great influence on me.'*
**Brian May**

A few days later, after I've walked Molly in the park and she's sleeping happily on her bed, I check the dinner; chicken, mushroom and leeks with brandy, Dijon mustard and crème fraîche. The crispy rosemary and garlic roast potatoes are sizzling in the pan.

I've already baked Tina her favourite fruit cake to take to Graham's parents' home for lunch tomorrow.

It's kept my mind off the past few days and the aftermath of the events surrounding the capture of Anthony Bryant. It's made the news headlines around the world. It's been on TV channels, and journalists have reported live from The Cockerel and the Guinea Pig in Kent. If the pub wasn't well-known before, it certainly is now. The only difference is that it's closed and Daniel Clarkson has gone into hiding from the public. Social media speculation hints that it's very likely he's gone abroad. The paparazzi have interviewed his wife, Jenny, and she's determined to reopen it very shortly and is taking bookings for Christmas. I like what I've read of her, and I'm pleased.

The doorbell rings and Tina comes in armed with two bottles of Bollinger.

'Oh my goodness, Ronda. You have been in the wars.'

I touch the cut above my bruised eye.

'Well, at least the others came off worse.'

I grin. I'd given her a detailed account last Wednesday night after I got home and she's telephoned me every day since, to check on how I am. She thrusts a brown paper bag at me.

'I thought you'd need some new ones after all that excitement. Have you seen the news?'

'I've given up watching it.'

I open the bag, and six colourful bandanas slide out. They are multi-coloured, patterned, rainbows, prints and flowers. 'These are beautiful, thank you.'

'Do you hear what's happened today?'

'No.'

'Lord Bonner committed suicide this morning.'

I sit down at the table, shocked. 'Why?'

'The report said he couldn't take the shame of any more bad publicity. He thought that this deal would save him, and it might renew some favourable public opinion, but once the truth came out last Friday about the INTmon scandal, he couldn't take any more.'

'I thought he was more arrogant than that.' I remember how he'd been speaking on his phone in the bar.

'He had it lined up to float on the stock exchange.'

'I don't know how they thought they'd get away with it. Detectives monitor cryptocurrencies all the time on the Internet.

A few months ago, they found a lot of mule bank accounts. They were using them to transfer cash on behalf of other people to invest in a similar scheme, only this one involved lending money to people.'

'Money laundering?' I ask.

'Complete and utter fraud. Luckily the Met Police managed to retain over £100,000 of cryptocurrency and the gang went to prison.'

'I'm sorry for all of them. I'm even sorry for Lord Bonner and his family; I blame James. He's the one who put this all together. He certainly groomed Nina.'

'And he will go to prison, I'm sure.' Tina pulls off the wrapper and pops the cork on the bottle.

'You sound like an international criminal lawyer.'

Tina grins. 'Where are the glasses?'

'In the freezer, nice and cold.'

'Then get them because we're celebrating.'

I grin. 'I've made your favourite dinner.'

'I know, and it smells delicious.'

There's a glow to her today, a special aura of excitement. I pull out the glasses and place them on the table.

'Have you been following the case? Is this what we're celebrating?' I ask.

She shakes her head, and when she waves her fingers under my nose, she flashes a large diamond engagement ring at me.

'Graham's proposed.'

* * *

I don't pluck up the courage to visit Hugo until Sunday afternoon. I stop to buy him dried sunflowers and some ripe black grapes and make my way to the reception of the private wing in the Chelsea hospital. I ask for Hugo's room and, as I wait for the lift, Inspector Joachin appears. He's walking down the stairs and he smiles and kisses me in greeting.

'I'm just leaving.'

I nod. 'How is Hugo?'

'He'll be fine, but I did want to speak to you, Ronda. Do you have a few minutes?'

He doesn't wait for me to answer. Instead, he leads me gently by the arm to the chairs near the window. I glance outside, where the lights are coming on along the embankment. There's a festive feel already outside; shoppers, traffic and lights.

'We have managed to keep your name out of the papers, but you will have to testify in court.'

I nod.

'I'm sorry, but we want to put James away for a long time.'

'That's fine. He deserves it.'

'I know it's not easy to testify against someone you once loved.' His eyes are dark, sincere and solemn, and he gives me a small smile before continuing, 'The police are pleased with your statement. You've behaved very professionally. Aiden has also spoken out in your favour. He said you were exemplary.'

'I'm pleased everyone was safe.'

'That's all down to you. Tony Bryant will be extradited to stand trial in America.'

'Everything worked out well then, apart from Hugo who was shot in the leg. That was a mess-up. I feel awful about it.'

'He's made a statement. It wasn't your fault. We know it happened while you were wrestling with the bodyguard. Tony Bryant had ordered him to shoot Hugo. So, if you think of it like that, then you saved Hugo's life. Goodness knows what would have happened if you weren't there, Ronda.'

I shrug. 'I still feel responsible. I should have protected him.'

He smiles. 'He's looking forward to seeing you.'

'Good.'

Inspector Joachin stands up, so I stand up with him, still holding the flowers and the grapes.

'Goodbye, Ronda George, you're a very remarkable and resourceful young lady.'

He kisses me on both cheeks and turns away.

He's only gone a few paces when I call out.

'Inspector Joachin.'

He turns.

'You told me not to go to the pub, was that deliberate?'

'We knew you'd be an asset, but we had to warn you.'

I smile, thinking of how they manipulated me while sitting in my flat and eating my cake and scones.

I tilt my head to one side and regard him carefully. 'You haven't asked me to work for you.'

'I didn't want to push my luck.'

'You should have.'

He smiles. 'Really?'

'Yes.'

'Would you like to work with me, with us, in the future?'

'Yes, please.'

'Why the change of heart, Ronda?'

'Because I've got my mojo back again. As much as James destroyed me and took everything, ironically standing up to him and ruining his crooked plans has made me feel much better about myself.'

'Good.'

'Besides, I think I'll be a good asset to your team.'

241

Inspector Joachin nods. 'I know you will be.'

\* \* \*

Hugo's room is quiet, and there's a light on above his bed so that he can read. He puts down his book and looks up.

'Well, at last! My saviour is here at last. I hoped you'd visit me.'

'Here.' I place the flowers on the table over his legs. There's a massive bouquet on the cabinet.

'Who are these from?' I ask.

'Prince Abdul. He's gone back to South America.'

'How lovely.' I put the fruit in front of him, and it looks paltry compared to the bowl of cherries, ripe peaches, apples and oranges.

'I suppose the fruit is from him too?'

Hugo smiles.

'But my grapes have medicinal powers, they will cure you,' I say.

'A likely story.'

I sit in the empty chair beside the bed. 'So, how long are you going to milk this for?'

He turns down the corners of his mouth. 'I hoped for at least another week in bed reading quietly with nothing to do, but it looks like they're sending me home tomorrow.'

'So you're not going to die?'

'Not this time.' He grins.

His eyelashes are dark, and his eyes look tired.

I take a deep breath. 'I'm sorry I left you for so long in the cellar.'

'It's not your fault.'

'I told Daisy to get the police. I sent her to the village, but I guess if Daisy hadn't—'

He holds up his hand.

He says, 'She phones me every day and she keeps apologising for not going to the village the first time and for the fact her phone ran out of battery. I keep telling her it's not her fault. Can you speak to her, please?'

'She phones me twice a day too,' I reply. 'I even told her that she saved your life but she's not interested, sorry. She keeps asking me to relay the conversation I had with Gloria when I asked her for a signed photograph. Gloria is much more important than you are now you're going to live. I think she's checking to make sure I'm not lying and I don't change the wording of my story.'

Hugo laughs. 'Daisy told me too. I can't believe that with all that going on, you packed Nina and Gloria up with desserts before they left. How cool is that?'

I grin. 'I'm a chef, remember?'

'You're more than that. You're a ninja warrior. I'd hate not to be on your side.'

'Well, you will be on my side. I've just seen Inspector Joachin downstairs and I told him I'm available for more work.'

Hugo smiles. He looks genuinely happy. His hair has grown longer, and there's a dark shadow on his skin as if he's growing a beard. 'Well, I might be out of action for a while, but with a little physiotherapy, I'll be back in no time.'

'Did you hear about Lord Bonner?' I ask.

'Yes. I've also had a message from Aiden Moore. He's a decent guy, I like him. Don't you think he looks like Idris Elba?'

I smile. 'He's asked me out for dinner. He's flying back to London for a few days before Christmas.'

'You should go, Ronda.'

'I might.'

'Nina sent me a *Get Well* card.'

I nod. 'She wants me to meet her agent.'

'Are you interested?'

'Maybe.'

'Joachin told me that Prakash has returned to India, and Enrique is back in Spain, but he's willing to testify against James, Tony and Magda.'

'Good.'

'Only in return for us dropping the charges against him for sale of black market goods.'

'Ah, not so good.'

'It's probably worth it. Magda is pleading that she didn't realise that it was all a fraud. She'd been working on the blockchain, and she wasn't happy because until last Wednesday she didn't know it all hinged on the development of the financial records for INTmon. Presumably, she was furious with James and Tony, but I guess it will be up to the courts to decide.'

'Is her name down as a director?'

'They can only trace the paperwork back to one of Tony's off-shore companies. They found he'd registered a bogus company through one of his companies in Nigeria. There's no paperwork leading back to Magda.'

'They've worked quickly on collating this information.'

'The police have been after him for years.'

'Maybe Magda's smarter than him, and she had more sense? How did she ever get involved with him?'

'Presumably, he's very good at networking. He has several people like James, who front his illegal businesses.'

'James will probably plead innocent.'

'Well, Tony won't be able to do that. He will be extradited to the US in the next few weeks, along with his two security men. He's wanted for drug smuggling. He's organised a drugs cartel for years.' His eyes darken. 'When Aiden came in yesterday, he told me he was aware of it, and that's why, when he saw Tony on Wednesday, he didn't want anything to do with this project.'

'Is he holding anyone to account for tying him up upstairs in the flat?'

'No, Prakash's bodyguard was doing his job. He's from an agency, and he'd been told to keep guard, nothing else.'

'They should have just let Aiden leave, but James is a control freak.' I pick up a grape and eat it.

'He said he knew nothing about Aiden being held captive upstairs.'

'He's lying,' I reply.

'James put a lot of pressure on Daniel,' Hugo agrees. 'And, that's probably why Daniel has gone into hiding. But on a brighter note, I think all the celebs will get their money back eventually. Their celebrity status isn't affected by any of it, and they are still the biggest influencers in the crazy world of social media.'

Hugo leans back and closes his eyes. He's tired.

'I'll leave you in peace.' I stand up.

'Good to see you, Ronda. And, thanks. I hope your eye gets better soon.'

'I'll probably be scarred for life because of you.'

'I'll have it on my conscience. I won't be able to rest.'

'Good.'

A tall, elegant man with bleached blond hair and a short beard walks into the room. He's dressed in trendy jeans and a thick hoodie.

'Hi, are you a friend of Hugo's?' He has an Australian accent.

'I'm Ronda.'

'I thought you were. I've heard so much about you. I'm Paul.' His smile is genuine and friendly.

'Paul,' I repeat.

'Hugo's husband.'

\* \* \*

I leave the hospital and head to the embankment where yellow lights on the opposite side of the river look warm and inviting. The Christmas market has opened today and it's busy with early shoppers. I lean on the wall and look across to the London Eye, thinking of Tina and how she flashed her engagement ring at me. She's seriously in love with Graham, and she's already asked me to be her chief bridesmaid next year – as well as organising the catering.

My mind drifts to Hugo and Paul in the hospital behind me. And the way they looked at each other, with kindness, love, appreciation and respect. Paul was charming and polite. He made Hugo laugh, and there was a mirroring of their behaviour and mannerisms that come when couples are in complete harmony. I'm happy for them. Just as I am for Tina and Graham; after all the excitement of the past week, life goes on.

'Maybe I'm fated to live alone,' I whisper into the cold night, and I begin to walk with my hands shoved deep into my pockets, and my chin tucked into my collar.

I miss Molly. I want to go home. I could feel depressed, but

I'm not. James is in prison. I don't care how he met Tony or Magda or how he groomed and persuaded the influencers. But he will have his day in court, and I'll be there in the witness stand, to tell the truth, and to see that justice is done.

My phone rings and I pull it out.

'Ronda, what are you doing on the fifth of December?'

'Hello, Daisy.'

'You'll never believe it, but I've just had a special delivery of four VIP tickets to Gloria's concert at the O2. You know she's doing a five-night tour, and it's the last night. She sent me a personal message – and, she's invited me backstage. She even sent a signed photograph.'

'Yay.' I grin and punch the air with my fist. Still smiling, I take a deep breath and contemplate the London skyline, feeling happier than I have in years.

'So, you did speak to her. I thought you were joking, Ronda.'

'I told you I spoke to her.' I laugh.

'Well, I want you to come with Hugo and me, and maybe someone else?'

'I know just the person that Hugo would like to bring.'

'Really?'

'Yes.'

'Great! Now, Ronda, tell me exactly what you said to Gloria. Where were you standing when you said ...?'


The End

# 20

# Want to read more?

**Read on for an extract: *The Manipulators***

## The Manipulators
*Book 3*

A Ronda George Thriller
Talented kickboxer and *Masterchef* turns detective.

*With lives at stake – time is running out...*

Ronda agrees to be the 'eyes and ears' for Inspector Joachin García Abascal from Europol, whilst catering for an international convention of 'Religious, Spiritual Minds and Bodies'.

At a remote monastery in Wales, the conference is thrown into disarray when tragedy strikes and a body is washed up on the beach.

But Ronda believes this is all a cover-up for a more serious crime - a sophisticated wine fraud.

As the truth is revealed Ronda must act quickly. She must use all her military training to succeed. But is she strong enough to stop an illegal and profitable crime when there's so much to lose?

The *Manipulators* is the third book in the Ronda George series of thrillers which can be read and enjoyed in any order, although it's exciting to watch Ronda's personal development with each book in the series and it's preferable to read them in sequence.

*For fans of female sleuths and aficionados of Lucy Foley, Catherine Cooper, Allie Reynolds, Shari Lapena, Riley Sager and Lisa Jewell.*

# 21

# The Manipulators - Chapter 1

*'Speculation is only a word covering the making of money out of the manipulation of prices, instead of supplying goods and services.'*
**Henry Ford**

I'm squinting at the rain, splashing solidly on the windscreen, as the wipers thud back and forth while checking the destination on my SatNav.

*You have reached your destination*, she announces.

I sigh. The drive from the country road, up to the imposing dark steel gates, on gravel, is bumpy and uncomfortable. Peanut, my Fiat 500, purrs to a halt while I survey the scene before me.

The monastery consists of an old stone Priory to my left, a small nineteenth-century church ahead of me, and a modern building called the Peace Centre, located on the Welsh hillside overlooking the wild and thrashing Irish Sea. Although it's not yet midday, it appears as though this is as light as the day will get, it's foggy with a dank, low grey cloud.

I pull down the window and the salty air rushes in.

From behind the gate, a monk appears in a dark brown habit. It's a loose-sleeved, hooded, gown and around his waist, a white cord is tied and hanging from that is a rosary. He waves and smiles. The gates open and I drive Peanut onto the tarmac drive.

'Welcome, to the Monastery,' the monk calls.

He's mid-forties and his hair is receding and grey. His jowls are flushed from the biting, cold December wind.

'You must be Ronda George.'

'Hello.' I give him the benefit of my best smile.

I haven't been this close to God since I was a child.

'I'm Brother John,' he replies. 'Welcome to St. Peter's. If you follow the gravel pathway to the back of the Priory, you can park there. You'll have to walk to the convent, but it's not far.'

'Thank you.'

'I'll follow you.'

'It's Baltic out there, do you want a lift?'

'No, no.' He smiles, he's already closing the gate behind me. 'I'm used to it.'

To my right, I pass a row of signs on the cliff tops with white circles and red lines:

*Danger. Do Not Pass. Beware. Caution.*

At the back of the Priory I park beside a small, maroon-coloured van with a St. Peter's Monastery emblem embossed on both sides. The logo is a swirling cross and two bloodied palms. It's the same logo as on the entrance gates and the notice board placed on the pathway leading to the main church door. Someone takes their marketing and branding seriously. They've done an excellent job.

As I pull to a stop and glance to my right, the magnificent and eye-catching logo is also above the entrance to the modern Peace Centre, a white building with long glass windows, that looks busy inside. The main hall is illuminated and seems to be a hub of activity and; I assume; this is where the weekend conference will take place.

The three buildings are in a triangle with St. Peter's Church at the pinnacle,where it overlooks the cliffs and the rough, dark, churning sea below. As I listen to the roar of the pounding waves on the rocks, it's dramatic and invigorating, and I slide the window shut.

I hadn't wanted to take this job so near to Christmas but after attending Gloria's concert last week - the famous Canadian chart-topper, and the last gig in her European tour at the O2, I knew I had to get my life back on track. Her music had filled me with vigour and energy, and I'd hummed along to her new chart-topping hit the whole way from London to the north-west corner of Wales:

*You will not bring me down, you will not make me your clown*
*I will stay true, I will not follow you*
*I am me.*

I climb out of the car and inhale the sea air, stretching my legs and arching my back. I rub my hands through my short hair, conscious that it's standing up on end, and it needs a cut. This would be a perfect location for a luxury hotel and a spa weekend, and if it were, I'd book in immediately and stay a fortnight.

The events from last month are still firmly in my memory. Although my cuts have healed and the bruising has faded, the emotion of coming face to face with my ex-partner who was about to pull off one of the most outrageous scams and earn himself billions of dollars still rages through me. Fortunately, James is now firmly behind bars with no chance of bail and waiting for his trial in the new year. I doubt I will ever get the money back that he stole from me - thirty thousand pounds - but I'm pleased I've been instrumental in stopping him, literally, with my bare hands.

Unfortunately, poor Hugo, a Europol police officer and my friend, had been shot accidentally in the thigh. He is now in physiotherapy and making good progress.

Behind me, the arched leaded windows of the stonewalled Priory is illuminated with yellow lights making it look warm and inviting. Still, I imagine it inside, a long wooden table with hooded monks hunched over mugs eating dry bread and drinking ale. I shake my head to rid it of the medieval images and think about this weekend's conference.

'Religious, Spiritual Minds and Bodies' – an international convention of medical doctors, monks, nuns, and a local prayer group.

I hear footsteps on the gravel behind me and I turn to watch Brother John hurrying toward me, his gown flapping in the wind, his hand outstretched.

'Ronda, it's delightful to meet you. I'm such a fan.'

Brother John is over a foot taller than me and his feet are bare in his open sandals. His grip is firm, and his large hands make mine feel small by comparison.

'I'll confess now, Ronda. I watched every episode of *Masterchef* and I loved the lemon meringue, it looked simply beautiful.' His voice is melodious and rich.

I smile. 'Thank you.'

The meringue had earned me a place in the semi-final that I'd gone on to win. It seems to be a dish that many people remember, or was it the fact that I'd punched the air in delight and almost knocked the host in the face? Either way, that's what many viewers remembered.

'How was your journey? The last weekend before Christmas is always a busy time on the roads.'

'I was lucky. I left early.'

'London can be a bit of a slog, especially on a Friday morning.'

'Five hours but I did stop on the way.'

'Good, good. Well, welcome to St. Peter's Priory. You're shivering. Come in and get warm. Let me help you with your bags, and then I'll take you over to the convent. It's the far side of the field, and it's quicker to walk. Sister Mary has agreed for you to stay both nights.'

'Thank you.'

'It's easier than you trekking back to a hotel in town each night.'

He stares, his eyes peering inquisitively into mine.

'You're much taller than I thought you'd be,' he adds.

'I've learned that television can be quite misleading.'

He grins. 'You've still got those unusual green eyes, though. My goodness, they're quite remarkable.'

He leans past me and reaches into Peanut's boot, lifting my weekend bags effortlessly. He's built like a wrestler, and I'm sure he is a solid body of muscle and, as he leads me inside, I wonder if the monks have their own private onsite gym.

'I'll let Sister Mary know you've arrived. If you think this is remote, wait until you see where they're located.'

I return his smile.

Inspector Joachin had warned me St. Peter's was isolated, but there's also something peaceful and calming about the place, and I'm struggling hard to reevaluate what he'd told me only two days ago. He'd arrived at my flat and, after paying Molly a suitable amount of attention, he'd accepted coffee and a large slice of carrot cake before asking for my help. He said, it wasn't a matter of life and death, but there was some serious fraud going on at the monastery. He said my task was simple. A weekend catering and to be his eyes and ears – at the conference. I had been unable to refuse his request. I'd tried to figure out why on the drive to Wales this morning. I could have said no. I could have refused. I could have made an excuse, but I hadn't. I had actually felt a quiver of excitement. A thrill of expectation. A desire for action. And the awful thought dawned on me; perhaps this business was addictive.

To read more click here.

# Janet Pywell's Books

**The Westbay Romance Series:**
Someone Else's Dream
Someone Else's Child
Someone Else's Truth

**Ronda George Thrillers:**
The Concealers
The Influencers
The Manipulators
The Ronda George Thriller Boxset - books 1-3

**Mikky dos Santos Thrillers:**
Golden Icon – *The Prequel*
Masterpiece
Book of Hours
Stolen Script
Faking Game
Truthful Lies
Broken Windows

**Boxsets:**
Volume 1 – Masterpiece, Book of Hours & Stolen Script
Volume 2 – Faking Game, Truthful Lies & Broken Windows

The Mikky dos Santos series are also available as audio books.

**Other Books by Janet Pywell:**
   Red Shoes and Other Short Stories
   Bedtime Reads
   Ellie Bravo
   The Novel Mentor

For more information visit:
   website: www. janetpywellauthor.com

All books are available online and can be ordered through major book stores.

If you enjoy my books then **please do leave a review** from wherever you purchased the book. Your opinion is important to me. I read them all. It also helps other readers to find my work.

Thank you.

# About the Author

Author Janet Pywell's storytelling is as mesmerizing and complex as her characters.

Janet writes gripping crime thriller novels that will keep you quickly turning the pages. The **Mikky dos Santos thriller series** is set in different locations throughout Europe while the **Ronda George thriller series** is set in unusual properties in the UK.

After the Covid pandemic Janet published the first book in the **Westbay Romance series**, *Someone Else's Dream* — a heart-warming, uplifting, feel-good novel about courage, integrity and friendship.

The other novels in the series will also leave you tingling with emotion.

Janet gained an MA in Creative Writing at the Seamus Heaney Centre at Queen's University, Belfast. She has a background in travel and tourism and she writes using her knowledge of foreign places gained from living abroad and travelling extensively.

In April 2022, Janet Pywell published her first non-fiction book: **Ten Simple Steps for Writing Your Book**.

Janet currently lives on the Kent coast.

**You can connect with me on:**

🌐 http://www.janetpywellauthor.com

🐦 https://twitter.com/JanPywellAuthor

📘 https://www.facebook.com/JanetPywell7227

🔗 https://www.instagram.com/janetpywellauthor

🔗 https://www.subscribepage.com/the_novel_mentor

🔗 https://www.subscribepage.com/the-westbay-romance-series

**Subscribe to my newsletter:**

✉ https://www.subscribepage.com/janetpywell

www.ingramcontent.com/pod-product-compliance
Lightning Source LLC
Chambersburg PA
CBHW070915120626
46546CB00001B/277